COVID-19 AND LABOR MARKETS IN SOUTHEAST ASIA

IMPACTS ON INDONESIA, MALAYSIA, THE PHILIPPINES, THAILAND, AND VIET NAM

DECEMBER 2021

ASIAN DEVELOPMENT BANK

ADB

Notes:
In this publication, "$" refers to United States dollars.
ADB recognizes "Vietnam" as Viet Nam.

On the cover: The COVID-19 pandemic had differential impacts across demographic groups, occupational and skill-level categories, and firms and businesses. Various groups were particularly vulnerable to the crisis because of the nature of their work, type of working arrangements, and other factors like migration status.

Cover design by Michael Cortes.

Contents

Tables, Figures, and Boxes

Tables

Figures

Boxes

Foreword

The coronavirus disease (COVID-19) pandemic has had a devastating impact on labor markets worldwide, including in Southeast Asia. For countries covered by this study—Indonesia, Malaysia, the Philippines, Thailand, and Viet Nam—this has been a crisis like no other.

At the outset of the pandemic in 2020, these countries managed to contain the virus relatively well, with some heterogeneity in their response. All countries implemented strict containment measures including lockdowns, workplace closures, and mobility and travel restrictions. While playing a crucial role in mitigating the health impacts, these measures however had important repercussions on labor markets. The high level of integration of these countries in the global economy meant that, in addition to domestic factors, international demand fluctuations and supply chain disruptions were also key channels through which the pandemic affected jobs and incomes in the region.

As mobility restrictions and workplace closures prevented labor reallocation—across sectors, from wage employment to self-employment, or from formal to informal employment—unemployment rates initially surged in Indonesia, Malaysia, Thailand, and the Philippines, and to a lesser extent in Viet Nam as well, while many other displaced workers exited the labor force. Job losses understate the true impact of the pandemic, however, because of major reductions in working hours and incomes for those employed. As economies reopened in the second half of 2020, the recovery of formal wage employment lagged behind that of informal work and self-employment. Young workers suffered a disproportionate amount of job losses, and women were more likely to exit the labor force following job loss than men. The crisis exacerbated growing inequalities in the region along the skills dimension, hurting low-skilled workers, but also middle-skilled workers whose jobs are already at risk from automation.

As the labor market impacts of COVID-19 across Southeast Asia have been unprecedented, so was the governments' response. Social assistance measures made up the lion's share of social protection response in these countries. The pandemic exposed significant social protection gaps associated with high and persistent informality across the region. It also provided an opportunity for countries to address these gaps and expand coverage to new beneficiaries and previously excluded groups. As recovery sets in, the focus of fiscal policy can shift more strongly from relief to stimulus, and from stimulus to structural investments that would promote sustained and inclusive growth.

Just as the prospects of a recovery seemed favorable by the end of 2020 in some countries, Southeast Asia suffered a major setback in 2021, as the Delta variant of the virus wreaked havoc against a backdrop of slow vaccine rollout. The crisis is not over. At the time of writing of this report, newly identified variants of COVID-19 such as the Omicron are spreading through the world, and vaccine coverage remains highly uneven. There are considerable downside risks to economic and labor market recovery. This study provides a detailed analysis of the pandemic's impact on labor markets in Southeast Asia since the onset of the pandemic. It gives initial evidence to identify priorities, constraints, and opportunities for developing effective policies and strategies in the recovery period and beyond.

Ramesh Subramaniam
Director General
Southeast Asia Department
Asian Development Bank

Acknowledgments

This study was prepared by the Human and Social Sector Division (SEHS) of the Southeast Asia Department (SERD) of the Asian Development Bank (ADB). Sameer Khatiwada, Souleima El Achkar Hilal, Rosa Mia Arao, and Ian Nicole Generalao are coauthors.

We are grateful to ADB colleagues Paul Vandenberg and Milan Thomas of the Economic Research and Regional Cooperation Department (ERCD) and Michiel Van Der Auwera of the Sustainable Development and Climate Change Department who peer reviewed the report and provided detailed comments to earlier versions of it. We also thank SERD colleagues Anna Fink, Henry Ma, and Dulce Zara, for their valuable input during the SEHS knowledge-sharing event on 7 July 2021.

The authors presented this study at the IZA-WB Jobs for Development Conference on 1–3 September 2021 and at the Boosting Decent Work for Inclusive Recovery Conference at the ADB Institute on 27–28 October 2021, during which conference participants shared helpful feedback. This study will also be presented at the American Economic Association's annual meeting (Allied Social Science Associations) to be held on 7–9 January 2022.

The SEHS study team worked closely with Arturo M. Martinez Jr., Pamela T. Lapitan, Melissa C. Pascua, Joseph Bulan, and Marymell Martillan of the Statistics and Data Innovation Unit of ERCD to obtain the latest labor force surveys. Several national statistical offices also provided valuable assistance, particularly Badan Pusat Statistik (BPS–Statistics Indonesia), the Philippine Statistics Authority, Department of Statistics Malaysia, National Statistical Office of Thailand, and the General Statistics Authority of Viet Nam. Mike Cortes designed the cover and typeset the layout of the report, and Tuesday Soriano provided valuable editorial assistance.

Finally, we are very grateful for comments, guidance, and support from Vice-President Ahmed M. Saeed, Director General Ramesh Subramaniam, and Deputy Director General, Winfried Wicklein.

Ayako Inagaki
Director
Human and Social Sector Division
Southeast Asia Department
Asian Development Bank

Abbreviations

ADB	Asian Development Bank
ADBI	ADB Institute
ALMP	active labor market program
ASEAN	Association of Southeast Asian Nations
COVID-19	coronavirus disease
EPR	employment-to-population ratio
GDP	gross domestic product
GNI	gross national income
GSC	global supply chain
ILO	International Labour Organization
IMF	International Monetary Fund
INO	Indonesia
IPC-IG	International Policy Centre for Inclusive Growth
ISIC	International Standard Industrial Classification
Lao PDR	Lao People's Democratic Republic
LFPR	labor force participation rate
LFS	labor force survey
MSME	micro, small, and medium-sized enterprise
NEET	not in employment, education, or training
OFW	overseas Filipino worker
PHI	Philippines
PPP	purchasing power parity
Q	quarter
SAP	Social Amelioration Program
SME	small, and medium-sized enterprise
THA	Thailand
UNICEF	United Nations Children's Fund
VIE	Viet Nam

COVID-19 Impacts and Labor Market Adjustment Patterns

Despite early success in containing the pandemic in 2020, Southeast Asian economies and labor markets were hit hard

In the first year of the coronavirus disease (COVID-19) pandemic, Southeast Asia managed to contain the virus relatively well compared with most other regions, but with some heterogeneity across countries. Within our sample of five countries, Indonesia, Malaysia, and the Philippines registered more cases per capita than Thailand and Viet Nam. All countries implemented strict containment measures including lockdowns, workplace closures, and mobility and travel restrictions. While playing a crucial role in mitigating the health impacts, these measures had important repercussions on labor markets. Beyond these domestic issues, the high level of integration of these countries in the global economy meant that international demand fluctuations and supply chain disruptions were also key channels through which the pandemic affected jobs and incomes in the region.

As mobility restrictions and containment measures prevented labor reallocation in the first half of 2020, unemployment rates surged, accompanied by massive labor market exits

The way labor markets were affected, and the type of adjustment that took place signified various elements—such as the scale of the COVID-19 shock, policy response and stringent restrictions, and international trade and linkages—at work and interacting with structural factors. Job losses peaked in the second quarter (Q2) of 2020, when containment measures were at their most stringent. As mobility restrictions and workplace closures prevented labor reallocation across sectors—from wage employment to self-employment, or from formal to informal employment—unemployment rates surged in Indonesia, Malaysia, Thailand, and the Philippines, while many other displaced workers exited the labor force. In Viet Nam, where the largest share of job losses in Q2 2020 consisted of agricultural jobs, the vast majority of job losses consisted of transitions out of the labor force.

Job losses understate the impact of the pandemic, however, because of major reductions in working hours for those employed

Job losses only partially accounted for working hour losses, as labor market adjustment also took the form of reductions in working hours, including working zero hours while still being in employment. The extent to which working hour reductions—the intensive margin of adjustment to the COVID-19 shock—were used by firms and workers varied across sectors and countries. We considered various potential factors affecting the reliance on intensive adjustment margins at the sectoral level, including the share of wage and salaried work in employment, firm size, the "teleworkability" of the sector based on its occupational structure, and the share of temporary workers in employment. We found evidence that sectors with large shares of temporary workers were more likely to resort to extensive adjustment margins (job cuts), and that the prevalence of permanent wage and salaried work was positively associated with telework potential. While large-scale support to firms and workers (through wage subsidies, furlough schemes, etc.) aimed to protect jobs and preserve employment relationships in many advanced economies, wage subsidies had more limited reach in Southeast Asia, largely due to high levels of informality.

Economies reopened in the second half of 2020, the recovery of formal wage employment lagged behind that of informal work and self-employment

As containment measures weighed heavily on economies and labor markets, most countries began lifting restrictions in Q3 2020. The third quarter of the year saw a rise in labor force participation and significant transitions back into employment, as many of those who had exited the labor force reentered. Unemployment rates declined, but remained well above prepandemic levels. Transitions into employment in the second half of 2020 consisted primarily of movements to own-account work, contributing family work, and informal work, reflecting a lag in the recovery of formal employment.

In 2021, labor market recovery, the prospects of which seemed favorable by the end of 2020 in some countries of the region, suffered a major setback

In 2021, the numbers of COVID-19 cases rose exponentially in many countries of the region, as the Delta variant of the virus wreaked havoc against a backdrop of slow vaccine rollout. In Q1 2020, the employment-to-population ratio (EPR) remained well below—or had fallen once again back below—its precrisis level. Specifically, the ratio remained below its precrisis level by 3.5 percentage points in the Philippines, 2.4 percentage points in Viet Nam, 1.5 percentage points in Malaysia, and 0.4 percentage points in both Indonesia and Thailand. Indonesia's labor force participation rate had dropped to its lowest point since the onset of the crisis. As the pandemic raged on in these countries, labor market conditions continued to deteriorate as indicated by Q2 2021 data available for Viet Nam.

Differential Impacts of the Pandemic

Youth were hit hard across the region, through disruptions in education and training, delayed school-to-work transitions, and a disproportionate share of job losses among young workers....

Young workers, who represent only 10%–15% of the workforce in Indonesia, the Philippines, Thailand, and Viet Nam, accounted for a disproportionate share (between 22% and 45%) of job losses at the height of the pandemic's impacts on labor markets in these countries in 2020. This is owing to their overrepresentation in sectors that were heavily hit like food and accommodation services, wholesale and retail trade, and "other services," and also because they were more likely to lose their jobs than adult workers in these same sectors. In most countries in our sample, the recovery of employment for youth lagged behind that of adults in the second half of 2020. By Q2 2021, the EPR for youth in Viet Nam had dropped by more than 12 percentage points compared with its precrisis level, and the youth unemployment rate had reached the highest point since the onset of the pandemic. In Thailand as well, youth continued to be heavily affected in 2021, with the youth EPR declining by as much as 2.9 percentage points, compared with 1.1 percentage points for adults in the first quarter of the year. The significant job losses experienced by youth, who already faced important labor market challenges in the region—as reflected in high youth unemployment and youth not in employment, education, or training (NEET) rates—were accompanied by other pandemic-induced difficulties such as disruptions to education and skills development, and delays in school-to-work transitions. The compound effect of these impacts can have significant long-term implications for the career and earning prospects of these youth.

... and women were more likely to exit the labor force following job loss than men

The extent to which women were more affected by job losses than men in the region varied across sectors and countries. In Thailand, for instance, women accounted for approximately 60% of Q2 2020 job losses and around 90% of manufacturing job losses. In all countries, and across virtually all age cohorts, women were more likely to exit the labor force following job loss, while men were more likely to become unemployed (with the exception of Viet Nam, where most transitions out of employment consisted of labor force exits for both men and women). This is partly due to a larger share of the care burden falling on women. Although many female workers reentered the labor market in the second half of 2020, labor reallocation patterns pointed to an "added worker effect," or "distress employment" whereby additional (female) family workers join the labor force to compensate for lost household income. The labor market reentry of women in the third quarter of 2020, largely into lower "quality," lower productivity jobs implies that although there is no evidence of persistent labor market detachment, the pandemic could nevertheless have long-term negative impacts on the working lives of women. As of Q1 2021, the EPR and labor force participation rate of adult women in Indonesia, Malaysia, the Philippines, and Thailand had surpassed their precrisis levels, while the corresponding rates for men remained well below their precrisis levels. In Viet Nam, both male and female EPR and labor force participation rate had fallen back below their respective precrisis levels.

The crisis exacerbated growing inequalities in the region along the skills dimension, hurting low-skilled workers, but also middle-skilled workers whose jobs are at the same time at risk from automation and reshoring

The heavy toll inflicted by containment and social distancing measures to services sectors such as retail and wholesale trade, food and accommodation, transportation, and personal services, hit low-skilled workers hard, along with middle-skilled workers in sales and service occupations. Disruptions to manufacturing and construction had a large impact on middle-skilled workers in crafts and related trades occupations, and on plant and machine operators and assemblers. The pandemic's impact on these occupational groups where the potential of remote work was limited—due to a heavy interpersonal or manual task content tied to a specific location—has added to the ways technology is driving inequality in the region's labor market. Additionally, there is evidence that the pandemic's interaction with technology may have accelerated trends such as digitization, automation, and nearshoring or reshoring, with major implications for skills demand in Southeast Asia. These trends point to an increasingly important role for active labor market policies (ALMPs) and skills development in the years to come.

Informal workers, self-employed workers, temporary and casual workers, and migrant workers were among the most vulnerable groups

Informal workers and own-account workers, who constitute a large segment of workers in highly affected sectors, were particularly vulnerable to the crisis. Informal workers suffered many job and income losses in the early stage of the pandemic, and self-employment was the source of household income most affected by the pandemic across Southeast Asia throughout 2020. Informal workers and self-employed workers are overrepresented among the region's poor and near-poor workers. Job and income losses can inflict scars on these workers, who have limited access to savings and may have to sell productive assets in the face of food insecurity. These categories of workers also intersect with that of workers in nonstandard forms of employment, including temporary and casual work, all of whom have limited job security and little if any social protection coverage.

Migrant workers—those employed in the region and those originating from the region—were also heavily hit by the pandemic and its associated restrictions on travel and mobility. Southeast Asia hosts over 10 million migrant workers, two-thirds of whom are intra-regional migrants, in addition to being a major source of international global migrant workers. In particular, the Philippines is the source country for over 6 million migrant workers worldwide, and Indonesia for another 4.6 million. Migrant workers are often on fixed term or temporary contracts and therefore suffer greater job insecurity. Aggravating their precarious conditions was the lack of clarity on whether they could access health and welfare systems in their host countries.

The crisis also had a differential impact on firms, based on size, export orientation, access to finance, and government support among others

At the height of the pandemic's impacts on the region's labor markets in Q2 2020, micro, small and medium-sized enterprises (MSMEs) were disproportionately affected by job cuts. Micro and small firms have less liquidity, and had more limited access to, or capacity to avail of, government support. Differential impacts across firms took place along other dimensions as well, such as export orientation or the dependence on domestic or international markets. In Thailand, for instance, while small MSME employment in manufacturing recovered in Q4 2020, large manufacturing firms continued to shed jobs. The same pattern can be observed in both Thailand and Viet Nam in the accommodation and food services, where after taking a major hit in Q2 2020, MSME employment recovered in the second half of the year, while larger firms less affected by job cuts early on, shed more jobs in the second half of the year, as disruptions to international tourism persisted.

Social Protection and Labor Policy Response

As the labor market impacts of COVID-19 across Southeast Asia in 2020 was unprecedented, so was the governments' response

To counter the pandemic's devastating impact on jobs and incomes, governments around the world reacted swiftly, announcing and implementing significant response measures, including fiscal and monetary measures. In Southeast Asia, the fiscal response packages varied across countries, based on the severity of the crisis' impact on jobs and incomes and on fiscal space available. Fiscal measures announced or implemented since the onset of the crisis ranged from 2.7% of GDP in Viet Nam to 18.8% of GDP in Thailand, with spending on social protection constituting between 65% and 91% of the fiscal response packages in our five countries. Most policy measures were announced in the early stages of the crisis, with countries implementing additional measures, extending the duration of programs, and increasing spending commitments over time, including through budget reallocations throughout 2020 and 2021.

Social assistance measures represented the lion's share of the social protection response in these countries

Because the social insurance infrastructure and coverage were limited in these countries, and because the pandemic's impact fell heavily on informal workers, poor and near-poor households, social assistance programs and large-scale cash transfer programs in particular, played an integral role in the social response. Key interventions across our sample countries consisted of massive horizontal expansion (increased population coverage) of existing programs, although new programs were also introduced and other measures involved the vertical expansion (increase in benefits) of existing programs. In general, the speed and timeliness of interventions were aided by the use of social registries or beneficiary databases from existing programs and electronic methods for benefit disbursement (electronic transfers into personal bank accounts, and through electronic vouchers or payment cards).

Social insurance measures benefited a small segment of formal workers, but the coverage of these policies remained limited, emphasizing the need to intensify formalization efforts

Social insurance, which has very limited reach in the region, also constituted a small part of the response. Social insurance programs, where they exist, target formal employees and as such had very low incidence (less than 4%) among the poorest quintile of the population in these countries. Social insurance response measures to COVID-19 were generally linked to existing measures and pertained to four social protection areas: unemployment insurance, health insurance, sick leave and employment injury, and contributory pensions. In many cases, these programs were extended to groups of workers who would not have been covered otherwise and those who would not meet eligibility criteria, including formal sector workers with insufficient contributions, return migrant workers, gig economy workers, and others. The limited social insurance coverage highlighted by the pandemic, has further emphasized the need to tackle persistent informality in these countries. Intensifying formalization efforts would help reduce the vulnerability of workers, and also expand fiscal space available for social protection.

Labor market policies have also played a key role in the response, with some form of wage and training subsidies implemented across all five countries

ALMPs including wage and training subsidies played an important role in country responses, although the scope and coverage of interventions differed significantly across countries. The highest coverage by labor market policies (in terms of targeted percentage of the workforce) in these countries was afforded by Thailand's informal workers subsidy program and Malaysia's employment retention program. The adequacy of benefits was generally higher for the more targeted policies. As technology, trade, and other megatrends continue to shape the region's labor markets, wider access to skills development and training will remain crucial to help displaced workers avail of decent work opportunities. ALMPs, including policies for reskilling and upskilling, will continue to play a critical role in mitigating inequalities.

The pandemic provided an opportunity for countries in the region to fill preexisting social protection gaps and expand coverage to new beneficiaries

Before the pandemic, Southeast Asia had significant social protection coverage gaps: a large share of workers, often informal, were neither covered by social insurance (targeting formal workers) nor social assistance (targeting the poorest and most vulnerable groups, including children and others not in the labor force). These gaps were further exposed and highlighted by the pandemic. All countries in our sample have attempted to fill these gaps, by extending social protection to vulnerable groups. For instance, in Thailand, policy responses targeted youth and informal workers. Migrant workers were also targeted in many policy responses, for instance, in the case of overseas Filipino workers (OFWs) in the Philippines, and return migrants in Malaysia and Indonesia, among others. In many countries as well, eligibility criteria for social insurance were relaxed to allow workers who would not have been otherwise covered due to insufficient contributions, for instance, gig workers.

Pandemic spending has narrowed the fiscal space available for sustained interventions, but the crisis is far from over in the region

The devastating impact of the Delta wave of the virus in Southeast Asia in 2021, coupled with slow vaccination rollout, has required further containment measures and derailed, or at least delayed, recovery. An acceleration of the vaccination process and more equitable access to vaccines are critical in the short term for economies to begin to recover. The longer the pandemic persists, the more difficult it is for governments to sustain interventions. A gradual phasing out of emergency measures must be coupled with greater investment in social protection infrastructure, to sustain inclusive growth and improve resilience.

As recovery sets in, the focus of fiscal policy can shift more strongly from relief to stimulus, and from stimulus to structural investments that would promote sustained and inclusive growth...

The pandemic and the real risks it poses to the region in the form of slower long-term economic growth and increased inequalities, have emphasized the need for fiscal policy to go beyond its countercyclical role, through increased investment in social protection and its infrastructure. As such, it would play a more redistributive role. Countries should implement strategies to expand the fiscal space they have available for social protection, primarily by mobilizing domestic resources. In particular, increasing revenues from, and sustaining the progressivity of, taxation can provide positive spillover effects. Intensifying formalization efforts can also increase social insurance contributions and expand fiscal space for social protection.

... including by enhancing human capital development, improving quality and relevance of skills development and strengthening social protection systems

Key challenges for the Southeast Asian countries are to leverage achievements and lessons learned and innovative approaches used to respond to the pandemic (for instance, through the use of digital technology and e-banking) and channel the efforts to temporarily fill social protection gaps toward building more comprehensive, inclusive, and sustainable social protection systems. Additionally, countries must augment their investments in human capital, ensuring wider access to education and skills development and bridging the digital divide. Addressing these challenges must be a priority—not only to reduce vulnerability to shocks as emphasized by the pandemic—but to mitigate widening inequalities in labor market outcomes and living standards across and within countries.

Chapter 1

COVID-19 Impacts and Labor Market Adjustments

1 Key Findings

In the decade preceding the coronavirus disease (COVID-19) pandemic, employment growth fell short of working-age population growth in some Southeast Asian countries.

Despite significant progress, many workers remained in the poor and near-poor categories, and informal employment remained widespread across labor markets in the region.

The severity of COVID-19 impacts on Southeast Asian economies and labor markets depended on various contextual factors such as the effects on health, stringency measures, and the economic and labor market structure.

The impact of the pandemic was unprecedented, partly due to strict containment measures affecting sectors that would normally absorb displaced workers and preventing labor reallocation in the first half of 2020.

The peak of the crisis in Q2 2020 highlighted massive job losses and labor force exits, and major working-hour losses for those still employed.

In response to the crisis, intensive adjustment margins (resorting to reduced working-hours instead of job cuts) were used in varying levels across the different sectors and across countries in the region.

Labor reallocation occurred over the second half of 2020 as economies reopened, and a partial employment recovery was led by self-employment and informal work in Q3 2020.

The recovery of formal employment lagged behind that of informal employment, but generally took place in Q4 2020.

A renewed wave of the virus and slow vaccine rollout have set back the region's recovery in 2021.

COVID-19 hit Southeast Asia most severely in Aug–Sep 2021, as cases surpassed 2020 levels before winding down in Oct 2021

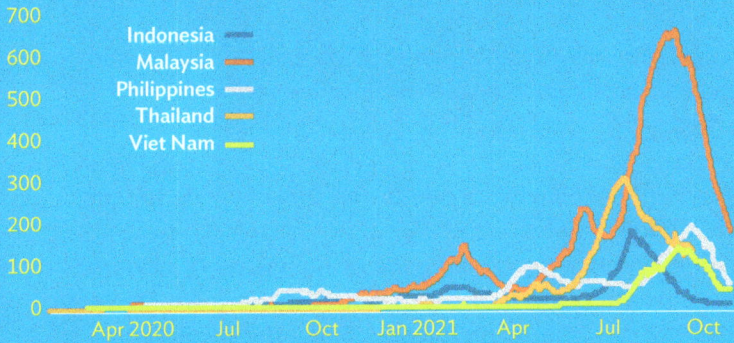

Indonesia
Malaysia
Philippines
Thailand
Viet Nam

700
600
500
400
300
200
100

Apr 2020   Jul   Oct   Jan 2021   Apr   Jul   Oct

Note: Shown is the 7-day rolling average.
Source: Our World in Data. COVID-19 Data Explorer.

Cumulative confirmed COVID-19 cases climbed from **1.3 million** at the end of 2020 to **12.2 million** by Oct 2021, and total deaths from **30,000** to **250,000**

Share of fully vaccinated population, by Oct 2021

Vaccination campaigns have accelerated, but coverage remains low except in Malaysia

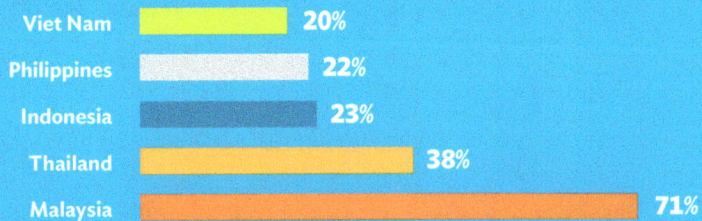

Viet Nam	20%
Philippines	22%
Indonesia	23%
Thailand	38%
Malaysia	71%

The Philippines had the most displaced workers and Thailand the least

Philippines

Viet Nam

Indonesia

Malaysia

Thailand

Among those who lost jobs...

52% became unemployed in the Philippines

... as many as **91%** in Viet Nam and **58%** in Indonesia exited the labor force

... while the majority in Malaysia **(61%)** and Thailand **(86%)** became unemployed.

Job gains over the second half of 2020 comprised mainly informal jobs and self-employment

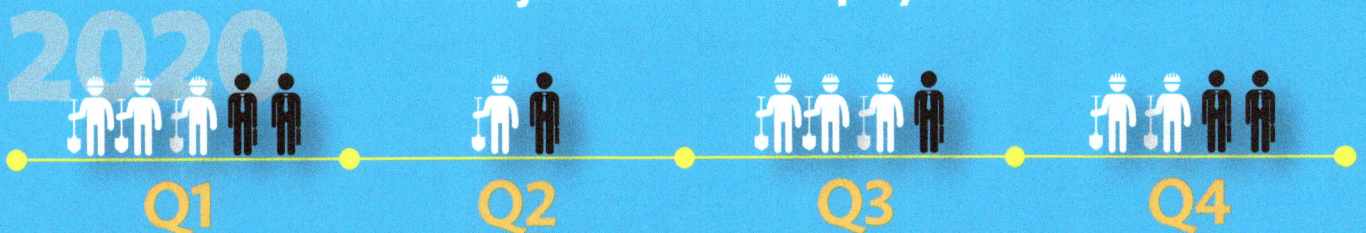

2020

Q1   Q2   Q3   Q4

The coronavirus disease (COVID-19) crisis hit economies hard, across Southeast Asia. Labor market adjustment to the crisis was unprecedented, as measures to contain the virus affected the sectors that would normally absorb displaced workers and prevented reallocation toward these sectors, at least initially. But some labor reallocation took place in the second half of 2020 as economies reopened.

This chapter provides a detailed account of COVID-19 impacts and the labor market adjustment process, focusing on five Southeast Asian countries—Indonesia, Malaysia, the Philippines, Thailand, and Viet Nam. Section 1.1 describes the labor market situation and trends in Southeast Asia before the pandemic. Section 1.2 examines the channels through which the COVID-19 pandemic affected labor markets in the region as well as labor market adjustment in terms of the transitions across labor force status (between employment, unemployment, or inactivity) over time at the aggregate level. Section 1.3 looks at labor reallocation (transitions *within* employment) to identify the extent to which this type of labor market adjustment mitigated job losses. Finally, section 1.4 decomposes the working-hour reductions at the sector level to analyze the intensive margins of adjustment to the COVID-19 shock.

Southeast Asia's Labor Markets Prepandemic

Despite relatively high gross domestic product (GDP) growth between 2010 and 2019 in most Southeast Asian economies, employment growth has been slow. In some countries such as Thailand and the Philippines, employment growth fell short of working-age population growth, and the employment-to-population ratio has declined steadily (Figure 1.1). Part of the decline in these countries, however, reflected lower labor force participation among the youth due to increased schooling. Nevertheless, the share of youth who are not in employment, education, or training (NEET) remained high in 2019, particularly among the females. Unemployment was essentially a youth issue in the region, with major gender gaps in labor market outcomes seen in some countries. Chapter 2 describes in more detail the disadvantaged position of youth and women in the region's labor markets.

While Southeast Asia has made significant progress in poverty reduction over the last decade, informality and working poverty remained widespread across many countries before the COVID-19 crisis. A large number of workers and their households still lived below or just above the poverty line, particularly in the low-income countries of the region (Figure 1.2B). In Cambodia, the Lao People's Democratic Republic (Lao PDR), and Indonesia, the share of workers living with their families below the poverty line (with an income of less than $3.20 in purchasing power parity [PPP] terms per day), declined by 24–27 percentage points between 2010 and 2019 (Figure 1.2A). In Cambodia, in particular, working poverty reduction consisted entirely of a decline in extreme poverty (share of workers living with their families below the $1.90 PPP per day threshold). The working poverty rate declined by 14 percentage points in the Philippines, and 12 percentage points in Viet Nam during this period. Additionally, the share of workers living in near poverty (between $3.20 PPP and $5.50 PPP per day) in Viet Nam declined by 18 percentage points. In Malaysia and Thailand, working poverty at the international poverty lines was virtually eradicated by 2019, but the poverty headcount ratio at the national poverty line was 5.6% and 9.9%, respectively, in 2018.[1]

---

[1]   World Bank. World Development Indicators. https://databank.worldbank.org/source/world-development-indicators (accessed 27 May 2021).

Figure 1.1: Evolution of the Employment-to-Population Ratio, 2010–2020

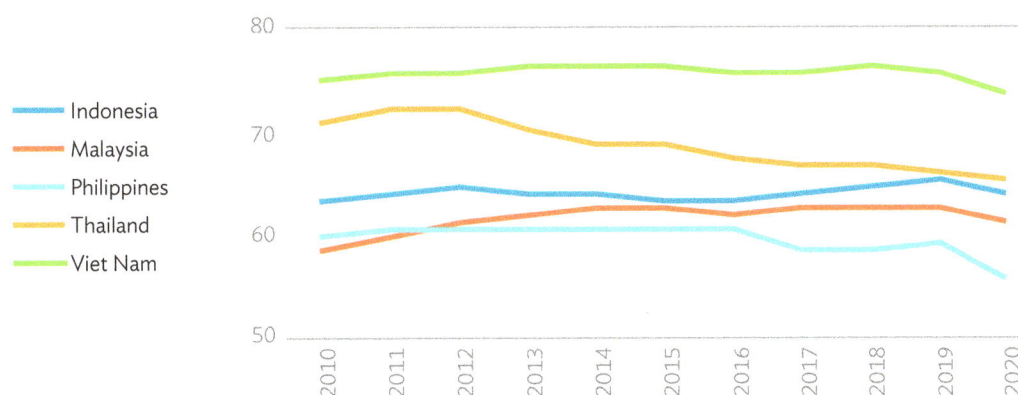

Legend:
- Indonesia
- Malaysia
- Philippines
- Thailand
- Viet Nam

Source: International Labour Organization (ILO). ILOSTAT. ILO modeled estimates. https://ilostat.ilo.org/data/ (accessed 22 October 2021).

Figure 1.2: Working Poverty in Selected Southeast Asian Countries, 2010–2019

A. Change in Working Poverty, 2010–2019
(percentage points)

B. Working Poverty Estimates, 2019
(% of employment)

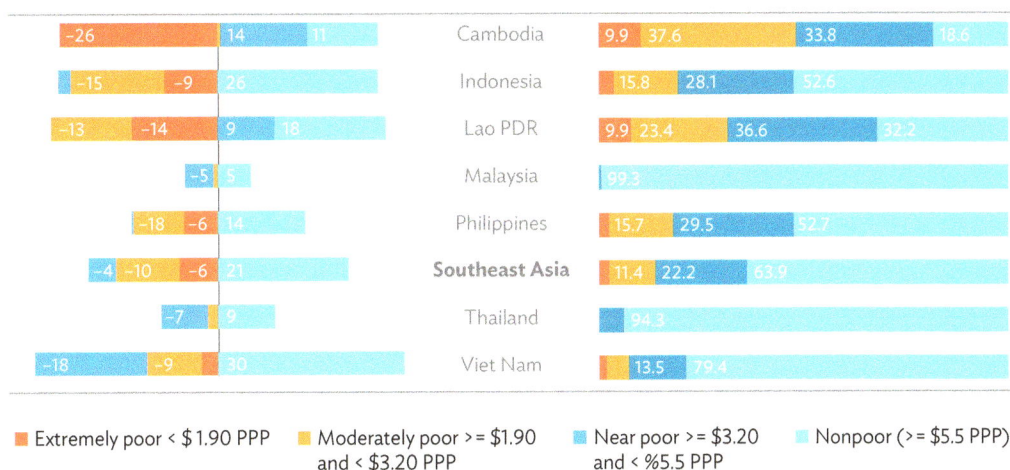

Country	A. Change in Working Poverty, 2010–2019	B. Working Poverty Estimates, 2019
Cambodia	−26, 14, 11	9.9, 37.6, 33.8, 18.6
Indonesia	−15, −9, 26	15.8, 28.1, 52.6
Lao PDR	−13, −14, 9, 18	9.9, 23.4, 36.6, 32.2
Malaysia	−5, 5	99.3
Philippines	−18, −6, 14	15.7, 29.5, 52.7
Southeast Asia	−4, −10, −6, 21	11.4, 22.2, 63.9
Thailand	−7, 9	94.3
Viet Nam	−18, −9, 30	13.5, 79.4

Legend:
- Extremely poor < $1.90 PPP
- Moderately poor >= $1.90 and < $3.20 PPP
- Near poor >= $3.20 and < %5.5 PPP
- Nonpoor (>= $5.5 PPP)

Lao PDR = Lao People's Democratic Republic, PPP = purchasing power parity.
Source: International Labour Organization (ILO). ILOSTAT. ILO modeled estimates. https://ilostat.ilo.org/data/ (accessed 22 October 2021).

Even in Southeast Asian countries with lower working poverty rates, informality in labor markets was high. The share of workers in informal employment across the countries in which these data were available ranged from 64% in Thailand to 94% in Cambodia, based on the latest year available.[2] Even when only nonagricultural employment is considered, workers in informal employment comprise between 52% in Thailand and 91% in Cambodia.

---

[2] International Labour Organization (ILO). ILOSTAT database [ILOSTAT explorer]. https://www.ilo.org/shinyapps/bulkexplorer32/ (accessed 14 August 2021).

Impact Channels, Aggregate and Sectoral Effects

Although the COVID-19 pandemic affected all countries, the scale and shape of its impact and corresponding labor market adjustment patterns have differed, driven by various contextual and institutional factors. Among the sample countries with available labor force survey (LFS) data, the crisis had the most severe effects in the Philippines, Malaysia, and Indonesia—at least in its early phases—with a period average of over 1,500 COVID-19 cases per million persons in each country between January 2020 and March 2021.[3] During this period, the stringency index for containment measures averaged 71 in the Philippines, 34 in Indonesia, and 62 in Malaysia.[4] Other Southeast Asian countries like Cambodia, the Lao PDR, Thailand, and Viet Nam had an average of less than 100 cases per million persons. Viet Nam's stringency index averaged (62), as high as that of Malaysia and Indonesia, while the average index of other countries with a similar range of COVID-19 cases (such as Cambodia, the Lao PDR, and Thailand) ranged from 39 to 47.

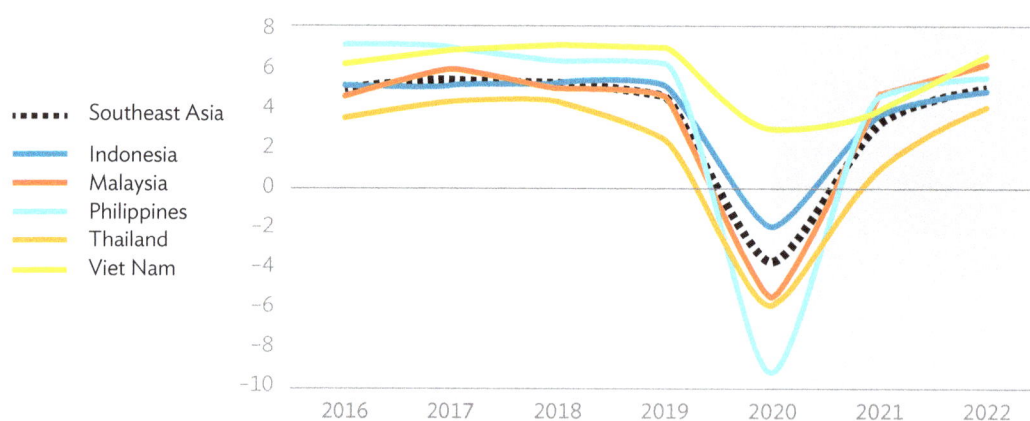

Figure 1.3: GDP Growth, Estimates and Projections, Selected Southeast Asian Economies, 2016–2022

Source: ADB (2021a).

The region's GDP growth dropped to –4.0% in 2020, with the Philippines experiencing the steepest decline (–9.6%), followed by Thailand (–6.1%) and Malaysia (–5.6%) (Figure 1.3). Viet Nam's economy proved the most resilient, maintaining positive GDP growth (2.9%) in 2020. By mid-2021, the COVID-19 situation in many countries in the region once again deteriorated, owing to slow vaccine rollout and new and highly contagious variants of the virus. As a result, Southeast Asia saw a downward revision in its growth outlook for 2021 (IMF 2021b). Nevertheless, most Southeast Asian countries are expected to have positive growth in 2021. The region's GDP is estimated to have increased at the rate of 3.1% in 2021 and is projected to grow by 5.0% in 2022.

---

[3]   Our World in Data. COVID-19 Data Explorer. https://ourworldindata.org/coronavirus (accessed 9 July 2021).

[4]   The stringency index was developed by Oxford University's COVID-19 Government Response Tracker, which measures the stringency of government measures imposed in response to the COVID-19 outbreak, such as school and workplace closures, travel and transport bans, stay-at-home requirements, and restrictions on large gatherings and public events. The value is scaled from 0 to 100 (100 = strictest).

Overall, annual net job and working-hour losses do not reveal the full extent of the labor market impact in 2020, because job and working-hour gains in the second half of the year partially offset the losses in the first half. For this reason, this report relies primarily on quarterly data to quantify the impacts and describe the adjustment process, examining flows across labor force status and transitions within employment (labor reallocation). The COVID-19 crisis led to significant net transitions out of employment, particularly in the second quarter (Q2) of 2020. For most countries, job losses and work stoppages were accompanied by significant exits from the labor force. Figure 1.4 shows the net movements of individuals between employment, unemployment, and in and out of the labor force from January 2020 to January 2021, overlaid with the number of COVID-19 cases and the stringency index for the five Southeast Asian economies.

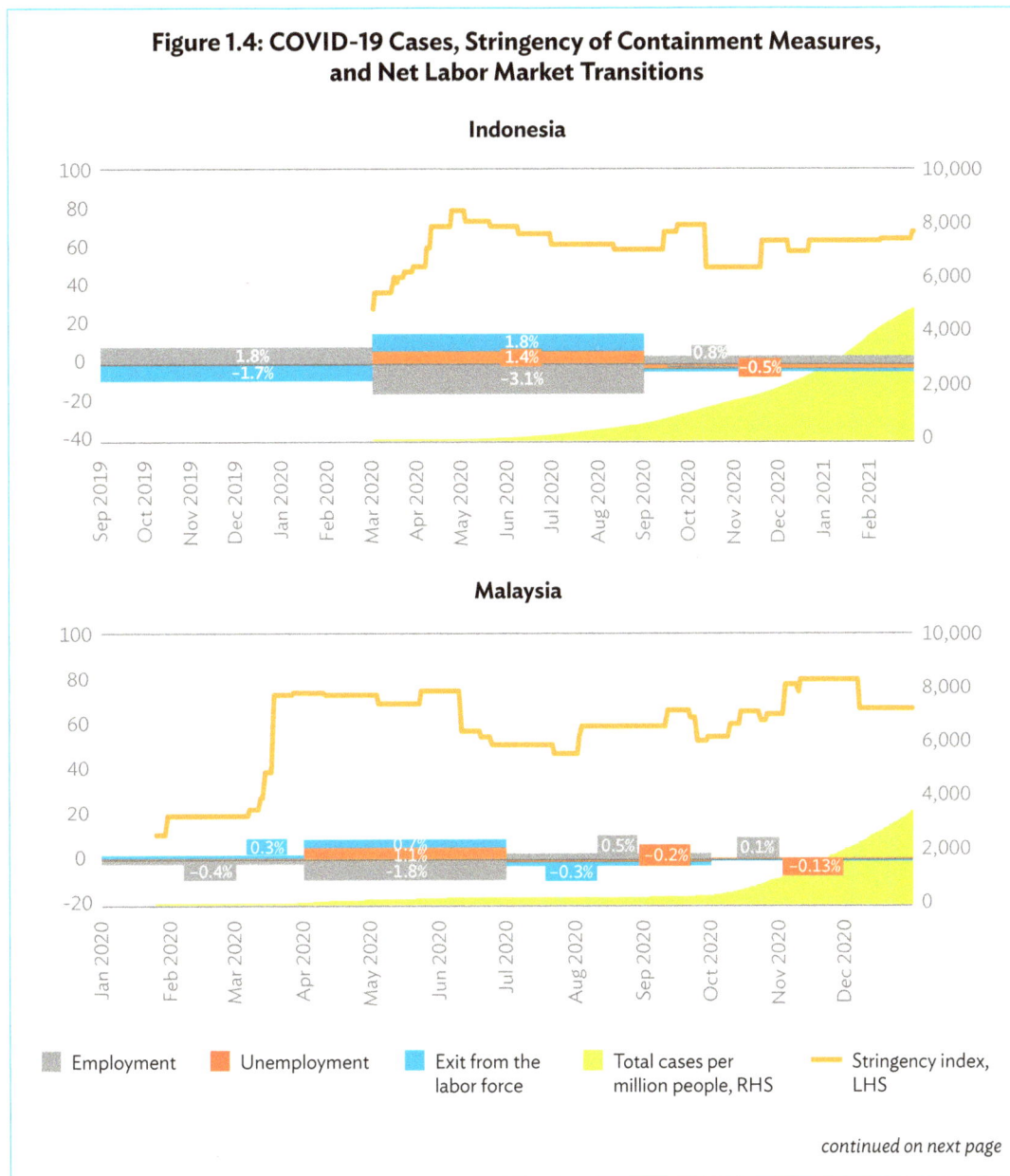

Figure 1.4: COVID-19 Cases, Stringency of Containment Measures, and Net Labor Market Transitions

Indonesia

Malaysia

Employment   Unemployment   Exit from the labor force   Total cases per million people, RHS   Stringency index, LHS

continued on next page

Figure 1.4 continued

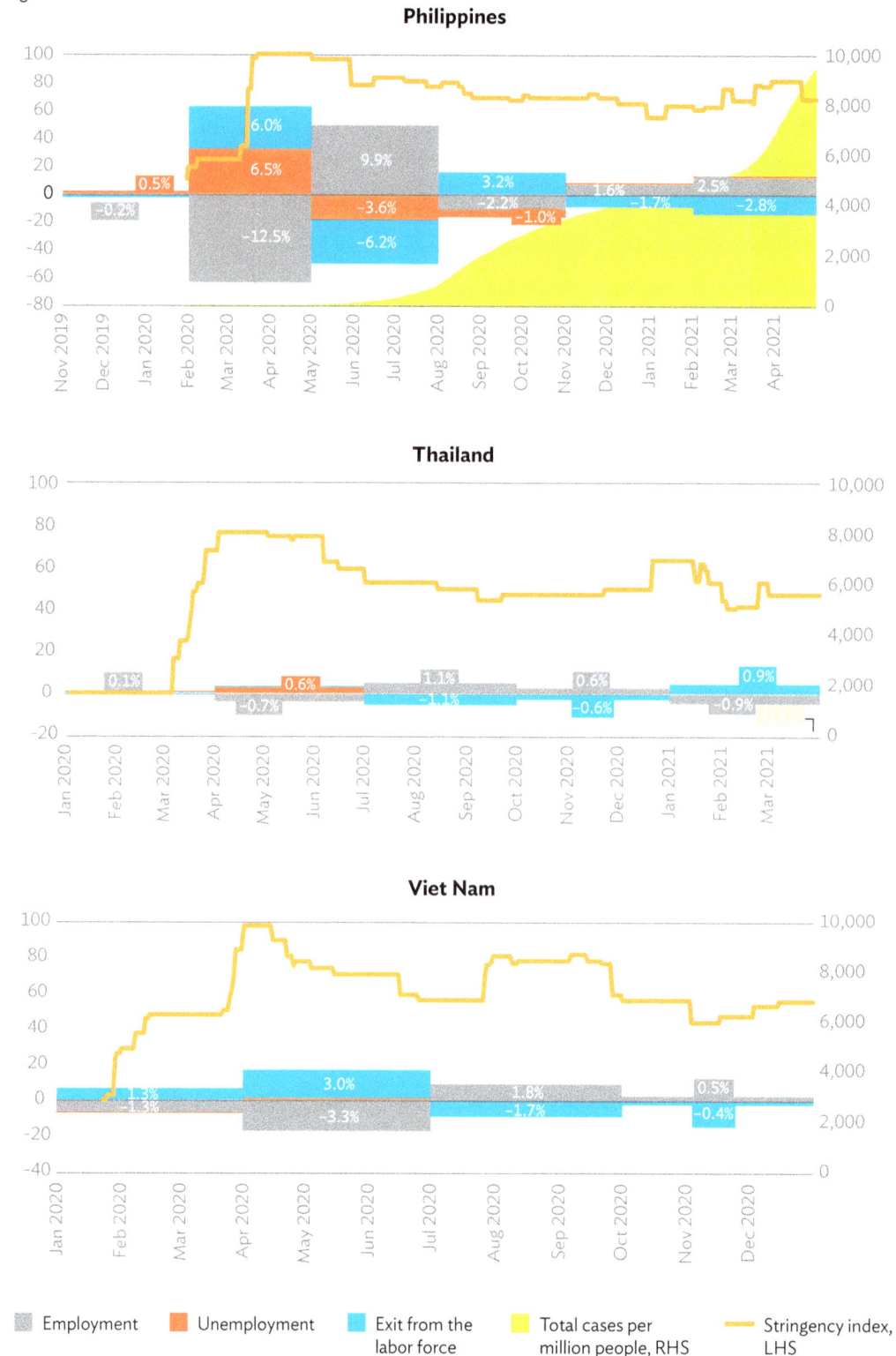

Philippines

Thailand

Viet Nam

Legend: Employment | Unemployment | Exit from the labor force | Total cases per million people, RHS | Stringency index, LHS

LHS = left-hand side, RHS = right-hand side.
Sources: Labor force surveys of various countries; Stringency index and COVID-19 cases from Our World in Data. COVID-19 Data Explorer. https://ourworldindata.org/coronavirus (accessed 9 July 2021).

The COVID-19 crisis has had highly sectoral impacts, hitting the hardest sectors that (i) were affected by supply chain disruptions and a decline in aggregate demand, both domestic and international; (ii) were affected by mobility and travel restrictions; and (iii) had limited possibilities of telework. At the peak of job losses in Q2 2020, manufacturing accounted for a large share of these losses in many countries of the region, with 27% in Indonesia, 22% in Viet Nam and Thailand, and 11% in the Philippines (Table 1.1, see also Box 1.1).[5] In Viet Nam, agriculture accounted for the largest share (46%) of job losses in Q2 2020. In all countries, the wholesale and retail trade sector and the accommodation and restaurants sector also reported a substantial share of job losses. In particular, the wholesale and retail trade sector accounted for nearly a quarter of job losses in the Philippines.

Table 1.1: Job Losses by Sector in Selected Countries, Q2 2020 versus Q1 2020

Sector	Philippines		Thailand		Indonesia		Viet Nam	
	Net Change in the Number of Employed ('000s)	Sector Share in Gross Job Losses (%)	Net Change in the Number of Employed ('000s)	Sector Share in Gross Job Losses (%)	Net Change in the Number of Employed ('000s)	Sector Share in Gross Job Losses (%)	Net Change in the Number of Employed ('000s)	Sector Share in Gross Job Losses (%)
Agriculture	-864	10	710		178		-1,126	46
Mining and quarrying	-30	0	7		10		-2	0
Manufacturing	-936	11	-237	22	-976	27	-525	22
Utilities	-60	1	-8	1	-37	1	-1	0
Construction	-1,210	14	-115	11	36		30	
Wholesale and retail	-2,131	24	-154	14	98		-153	6
Transport and storage	-805	9	-32	3	289		-97	4
Accommodation and food service	-778	9	-123	11	176		-154	6
Information and communication	-105	1	8		-409	11	-38	2
Financial and insurance	-189	2	-36	3	-13	0	-46	2
Real estate	-48	1	-23	2	-233	6	-44	2
Professional, scientific and technical	-37	0	-22	2	-28	1	-24	1
Administrative and support services	-162	2	-68	6	-11	0	-67	3
Public administration	-304	3	11		-762	21	2	
Education	-207	2	-84	8	-967	27	-99	4
Human health and social work	-106	1	-48	4	-173	5	-5	0
Other services*	-741	9	-128	12	252		-54	2
Net change	-8,713		-343		-2,570		-2,402	
Gross job losses	-8,713		-1,079		-3,608		-2,434	

* Other services include employment in (i) the arts, entertainment, and recreation; (ii) other service activities; and (iii) activities of households as employers. For Indonesia, changes refer to February 2020–August 2020.
Source: Authors' estimates based on labor force surveys of various countries.

[5] Manufacturing was hit hard across the region. In Cambodia, for instance, the sector is estimated to have accounted for approximately 25% of employment losses (ADB 2020).

Among the sample countries, the Philippines was the most affected in 2020 in terms of health outcomes (COVID-19 cases) and also in economic and labor market impacts. In Q2 2020, the highest transition out of employment accompanied the shutdown of all nonessential businesses beginning in mid-March until the end of May 2020 (Figure 1.4). One out of five workers (equivalent to 12.5% of the working population) transitioned out of employment, of which 6.5% became unemployed and another 6% exited the labor force. This translates into around 9.2 million workers leaving employment, with 4.8 million moving into unemployment, and 4.2 million leaving the labor force. The unemployment rate rose from 5.3% in Q1 2020 to 17.6% in Q2, and the labor force participation rate dropped by 6 percentage points during the same period (Table 1.2).

Table 1.2: Key Labor Market Indicators, Selected Countries , Q1 2019–Q2 2021

	Indonesia			Malaysia			Philippines		
	EPR	UR	LFPR	EPR	UR	LFPR	EPR	UR	LFPR
Q1 2019	65.8	5.0	69.3				57.0	5.2	60.2
Q2 2019							58.2	5.1	61.4
Q3 2019	64.0	5.2	67.5				58.7	5.4	62.1
Q4 2019				66.8	3.2	69.1	58.7	4.5	61.5
Q1 2020	65.8	4.9	69.2	66.4	3.5	68.8	58.4	5.3	61.7
Q2 2020				64.6	5.1	68.1	45.9	17.6	55.7
Q3 2020	63.0	7.1	67.8	65.2	4.7	68.4	55.8	10.0	61.9
Q4 2020				65.2	4.8	68.5	53.6	8.7	58.7
Q1 2021	63.8	3.9	66.1	65.3	4.8	68.6	55.2	8.7	60.5

	Thailand			Viet Nam		
	EPR	UR	LFPR	EPR	UR	LFPR
Q1 2019	67.1	0.9	67.8			
Q2 2019	67.1	1.0	67.8	74.3	2.0	75.9
Q3 2019	66.3	1.0	67.0	74.4	2.0	75.9
Q4 2019	66.3	1.0	66.9	74.5	2.0	76.0
Q1 2020	66.4	1.0	67.1	73.2	2.0	74.7
Q2 2020	65.7	2.0	67.0	69.9	2.5	71.7
Q3 2020	67.3	1.9	68.6	71.7	2.3	73.4
Q4 2020	66.7	1.9	68.0	72.2	2.2	73.8
Q1 2021	65.9	1.4	66.9	66.8	2.1	68.2
Q2 2021				66.5	2.4	68.1

"In 2021, recovery prospects suffered a setback, and employment levels remained well below or had fallen back below precrisis levels."

EPR = employment-to-population ratio, LFPR = labor force participation rate, Q = quarter, UR = unemployment rate.
Notes: The working population in Malaysia is 15–64 years old; in other countries, it is 15+ years old. For Indonesia, Q4 2019 is August 2019; Q1 2020 is February 2020; Q3 2020 is August 2020; Q1 2021 is February 2021. Data for Viet Nam in this table are based on the new standard definition of employment, consistent with the International Conference of Labour Statisticians 2019 recommendation. The EPR for Viet Nam differs from that in Figure 1.1, which presents the annual time series, based on the previous employment definition (standard ICLS 13).
Source: Labor force survey of various countries and International Labour Organization (ILO). ILOSTAT database [ILOSTAT explorer]. https://www.ilo.org/shinyapps/bulkexplorer32/ (accessed 1 December 2021).

Box 1.1: COVID-19 Impact on Manufacturing and Global Supply Chains in Southeast Asia

Over the past decades, Southeast Asia's importance in international trade and participation in global supply chains (GSCs) have grown with Malaysia, Thailand and Viet Nam transforming into major manufacturing hubs and key production zones for cars, computers, electronics and garments, among others (Mazumdaru 2021). GSCs in the manufacturing sector account for around 83 million jobs in eight countries of the Association of Southeast Asian Nations (ASEAN) or approximately 28% of total employment in these countries (ILO 2021d).

In 2020, the highly sectoral impacts of COVID-19 were reflected in massive disruptions to GSCs. At the global level, the number of GSC-related jobs experiencing high- or medium-adverse impact from the pandemic peaked at around 570 million in April 2020, declined between May and October 2020, but has increased again in the first half of 2021 (ILO 2021c). Supply chain disruptions heavily affected the garment and electronics industries—key industries of the manufacturing sector closely linked to GSCs in Southeast Asia. Both industries experienced delays in the production delivery time and cancellation of orders, resulting in failure to meet global and regional demand (ADB 2021b). In April 2021, an estimated 18 million and 35 million manufacturing GSC jobs in ASEAN member countries still experienced high- or medium-adverse impacts, respectively, as reflected in significant job losses, reduced working hours and income, and deterioration of labor standards and working conditions in the sector (see box figure).

Number of Jobs in Manufacturing GSCs Impacted by the COVID-19 Crisis in ASEAN

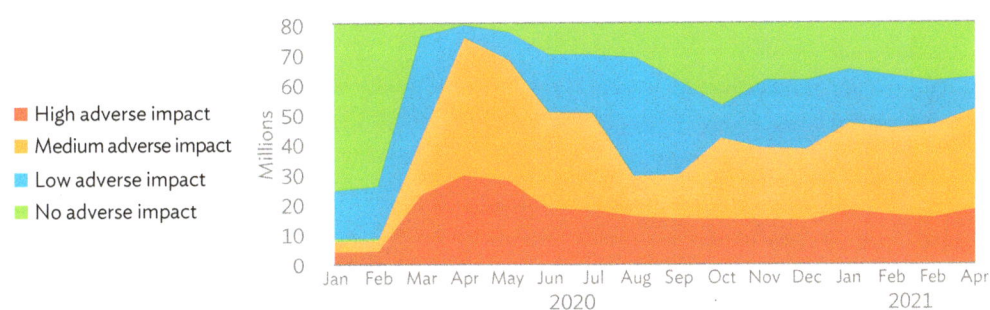

ASEAN = Association of Southeast Asian Nations.
Notes: The estimates shown include data for eight ASEAN countries (Brunei Darussalam, Cambodia, Indonesia, Malaysia, the Philippines, Singapore, Thailand, and Viet Nam). Estimates are derived from the methodology of ILO (2021c).
Source: ILO (2021d).

To counter the impact of the crisis, many firms restructured their supply chains to a certain extent to reduce cost and optimize resources, revised some of their relationships and agreements with clients and suppliers, and modified or considered modifying production locations—and most of these changes are unlikely to be reversed (Oikawa et al. 2021). In a survey of firms in GSCs across Southeast Asia and India, 40% of firms in the manufacturing sector had either restructured or planned to restructure their supply chains (Oikawa et al. 2021).

While it is early to ascertain how the pandemic has interacted with other trends shaping GSCs (such as technological change, shifts in consumer preferences, and sustainability) and whether it will accelerate reshoring or nearshoring, it has certainly revived the debate around these issues (see for example, European Parliament 2021; Richetti and Palma 2020), with potential implications for Southeast Asian labor markets. In any case, the COVID-19 crisis has exposed significant vulnerabilities of both firms and workers along supply chains, which must be addressed to improve the manufacturing sector's resilience as well as its contribution to creating decent work in the region, including for women who represent a large share of GSC workers in garments and other manufacturing industries in Southeast Asia (ILO 2020c).

Sources: ADB 2021b; ILO 2020c; ILO 2021c; ILO 2021d; Mazumdaru 2021; Oikawa et al. 2021.

Among the sample countries with quarterly LFS data, Thailand was the least affected in terms of employment losses, with only 0.7% of its working-age population exiting employment in Q2 2020. In net terms, only 14% of those who lost their jobs exited the labor force, thus leaving the labor force participation rate (LFPR) relatively unaffected (with only a 0.1 percentage point decrease). As a result, Thailand's unemployment rate doubled from 1.0% in Q1 2020 to 2.0% in Q2 2020.

In Malaysia, job losses had already started in the first quarter of 2020, but the second quarter registered the most significant exits from employment, equivalent to 1.8% of the working-age population. Among the workers who lost jobs, 40% exited the labor force and 60% became unemployed, raising the unemployment rate from 3.5% in Q1 2020 to 5.1% in Q2 2020.

In Indonesia, 3.1% of the working-age population (in net terms) transitioned out of employment between February and August 2020. Of these workers, 56% exited the labor force and the rest became unemployed, lifting the unemployment rate from 5.0% in Q1 2020 to 7.1% in Q3 2020.

Viet Nam was more successful in containing the pandemic than many other countries in 2020. But strict containment measures and other factors, including a decline in global demand, led to employment losses, which also peaked in Q2 2020, with 2.4 million or 3.3% of the working-age population. Of these workers, only around 220,000 (or 0.3% of the working-age population) joined the ranks of the unemployed, while the rest exited the labor force (as much as 93% of net job losses).

In Q3 2020, however, the easing of containment measures in the region led many of those who had exited to reenter the labor force, mainly transitioning into employment but with some becoming unemployed. Figure 1.4 shows a significant difference in the size of employment outflows in the early phase of the pandemic compared with the inflows during the "reopening" of the economy. In the Philippines, 9.9% of the working-age population moved back into employment, with 3.6% comprising people who moved out of unemployment into employment and another 6.2% making up those reentering the labor force (in net terms). Likewise, in Malaysia and Viet Nam, inflows back into employment in Q3 2020 fell short of the previous quarter's exits from employment and the employment-to-population ratio (EPR) and LFPR remained below their prepandemic (Q4 2019) levels. In Thailand, however, the number of those entering the labor force in the third quarter of 2020 exceeded those who had exited the labor force in the previous quarter, suggesting an added worker effect (discussed in greater detail in Chapter 2).

Restrictions continued to ease up in Q4 2020, and the year closed off with some countries having successfully contained the pandemic for most of the year.[6] Thus, in Q4 2020, a movement out of employment was observed only in the Philippines (2.2% of the working-age population) but to a lesser degree than the Q2 peak. In all countries, the unemployment rate had declined from its peak in Q2 but remained above its precrisis level, and the employment-to-population ratio below its precrisis level, throughout 2020.

In 2021, recovery prospects in Southeast Asia suffered a major blowback, with the number of COVID-19 cases rising exponentially in many countries of the region, as the Delta variant of the virus wreaked havoc against a backdrop of slow vaccine rollout. In Q1 2020, the EPR and LFPR increased in the Philippines, and very slightly in Malaysia, as the unemployment rate stayed constant in both countries (Table 1.2). In Indonesia, the unemployment rate declined in Q1 2021, as many

---

[6]   For example, Thailand recorded around 7,000 cases in a population of 70 million by the end of December 2020. Viet Nam had 1,465 total cases in a population of over 97 million.

unemployed exited the labor force, bringing labor force participation to its lowest point since the onset of the crisis. In Thailand and Viet Nam, however, Q1 2021 saw a decline in both employment and labor force participation rates. The unemployment rate declined as well in both countries, however, as many unemployed exited the labor force once again. In Viet Nam, the only country in our sample for which Q2 2021 data are available, the EPR declined further and the unemployment rate climbed back up in that quarter.

From September to October 2021, the number of new cases has trended downward and vaccination campaigns have accelerated, but coverage remains low with the notable exception of Malaysia. Although labor force survey data for the second half of 2021 are still unavailable, it is clear that labor market recovery, the prospects of which had seemed favorable by the end of 2020 in the region, suffered a major setback in 2021.

Labor Reallocation

In developing countries, the labor force participation rate is often high and the unemployment rate relatively low, because most working-age people cannot afford to be out of employment. Thus, in response to an economic crisis or shock, labor market adjustment occurs primarily through labor reallocation—shifts within employment, across economic sectors, across status-in-employment, or from formal to informal employment. The COVID-19 shock was unprecedented in many countries including in Southeast Asia, partly because lockdown and other containment measures heavily affected sectors that usually absorb displaced workers and prevented reallocation to these sectors.[7] For instance, sectors with high informality rates—such as wholesale and retail trade, accommodation and food services, construction, transport and storage, "other services," and even agriculture which usually absorb displaced labor from other sectors—accounted for 75% of the 8.7 million job losses in Q2 2020 in the Philippines, 65% of the 2.4 million job losses in Viet Nam, and 51% of the 1.1 million job losses in Thailand (Table 1.1).[8] In Indonesia, taking into account seasonal effects, employment in these sectors remained below precrisis levels, despite absorbing some of the displaced labor from manufacturing and other hard-hit sectors between February and August 2020 (Table 1.1, Figure 1.5). It is important to note that the February–August

---

[7] In comparison, during the global financial crisis (GFC), the employment-to-population rates of these countries (Indonesia, Malaysia, the Philippines, and Thailand) had declined by 0.3 to 1.0 percentage points in 2009 relative to 2008, and there were only slight increases in unemployment rates for some countries (e.g., Malaysia, the Philippines, and Thailand) ranging from 0.1 to 0.3 percentage points.

[8] In Viet Nam, however, construction sector employment increased in both Q2 and Q3 2020. In Thailand, the increase in agriculture employment in Q2 2020 followed an important decline in the previous quarter largely attributable to seasonal effects. It is nevertheless likely that some of the agriculture job growth in Q2 2020 consisted of displaced workers from other sections. Indeed, although net agricultural employment growth was positive in the sector in Q2, a shift can be observed from wage and salaried work to own-account and contributing family work within the sector.

INO

In Feb–Aug 2020, wage and salaried work declined by 10.5%, partly offset by increase in own-account work (11.4%) and contributing family work (6.2%)

VIE

89%

Between Q2 and Q3, informal employment (primarily in agriculture) accounted for 89% of net job gains (job recovery)

85%

Between Q3 and Q4, manufacturing employment recovered, formal employment made up 85% of net job gains

THA

Between Q2 and Q3, manufacturing employment declined further, within-sector employment shifts towards smaller firms in manufacturing and in food and accommodation

PHI

Between Q2 and Q3, large-scale labor reallocation toward wholesale and retail trade and agriculture

2020 time period includes several months of de-confinement and overlaps with both Q2 and Q3 for other countries with LFS data. During this period in Indonesia, a decline in employment for wage and salaried workers (–10.5%) and employers (–8.3%) was partially offset by an increase in own-account work (11.4%) and unpaid family work (6.2%).[9]

In other countries, some labor reallocation took place in Q3 2020 as the economy "reopened" and mobility restrictions were partially lifted. Movements into own-account work and unpaid family work explained much of the rebound in employment. This reflects a lag in the recovery of formal employment because of firm closures during the crisis, demand remaining depressed in sectors such as tourism, and continued uncertainty, which limit rehiring and investment. As a result, the COVID-19 crisis hampered the quality of work in these countries.

In Viet Nam, wage employment represented 47% of job gains in Q3 2020, with own-account work representing the remaining 53%. Most of the job gains (89%) consisted of informal employment, however, with agriculture jobs recovering from the major losses in Q2 and the wholesale and retail trade absorbing much of the displaced labor from other sectors. Taking into account seasonal effects, employment in agriculture and in accommodation and food services remained below precrisis levels at least through Q4 2020 (Figure 1.5). The construction sector also absorbed many displaced (male) workers in Q3 into wage employment. In Viet Nam, manufacturing and several key service industries saw a rebound in employment in Q4 2020 (Figure 1.5), and formal employment recovered, accounting for 85% of net job gains in that quarter. The last quarter of 2020 was marked by a shift back from self-employment to wage and salaried work, as many workers transitioned back from agriculture to the industry and services sectors.

In Thailand, most of the job gains in Q3 2020 occurred in own-account and contributing family work in agriculture. The manufacturing sector, which was the most affected in Q2 2020, continued to shed jobs in Q3. Most manufacturing job losses in both Q2 and Q3 were in wage and salaried employment, with larger firms—more likely to be export-oriented—reeling from the decline in global demand.[10] Despite some employment growth in Q4 2020, manufacturing employment remained below precrisis levels in Thailand (Figure 1.5). Employment in the badly hit tourism sector (proxied by accommodation and food services) in Q2 2020 recovered in Q3 2020 as economic activities resumed. In Q3, however, wage employment accounted for less than a quarter (24%) of the job gains in restaurants and accommodation, particularly in small and medium-sized enterprises, while the sector's larger establishments that rely more on global demand continued to shed jobs through Q3. In the last quarter of 2020, wage and salary work increased, particularly in sectors that were most affected in Q2, such as manufacturing, wholesale and retail trade, and education. The accommodation and food services sector continued shedding wage and salaried jobs in Q4, but posted overall employment gains as more workers moved toward self-employment (Figure 1.5). The slower recovery of wage employment in the tourism sector may be partly due to international demand remaining significantly curtailed as many western countries struggled with the second wave of the virus.

In the Philippines, we saw a Q3 2020 rebound in employment in agriculture, mining and quarrying, construction and wholesale and retail that matched or was higher than the job losses in Q2. A rise in self-employment and unpaid family work resulted in job gains in Q3 2020, with 24% of those gains occurring in wholesale and retail trade. In the last quarter of 2020, the Philippines posted a net job loss of around 1.5 million, tempered by the labor reallocation toward agriculture.

---

[9]   These figures refer to authors' calculations from quarterly LFS data. All supporting data can be found in Table A1.1.

[10]   The differential impact of the crisis by firm size is further described in Chapter 2.

Figure 1.5: Employment throughout 2020, Selected Industries
(Index, same quarter previous year = 100)

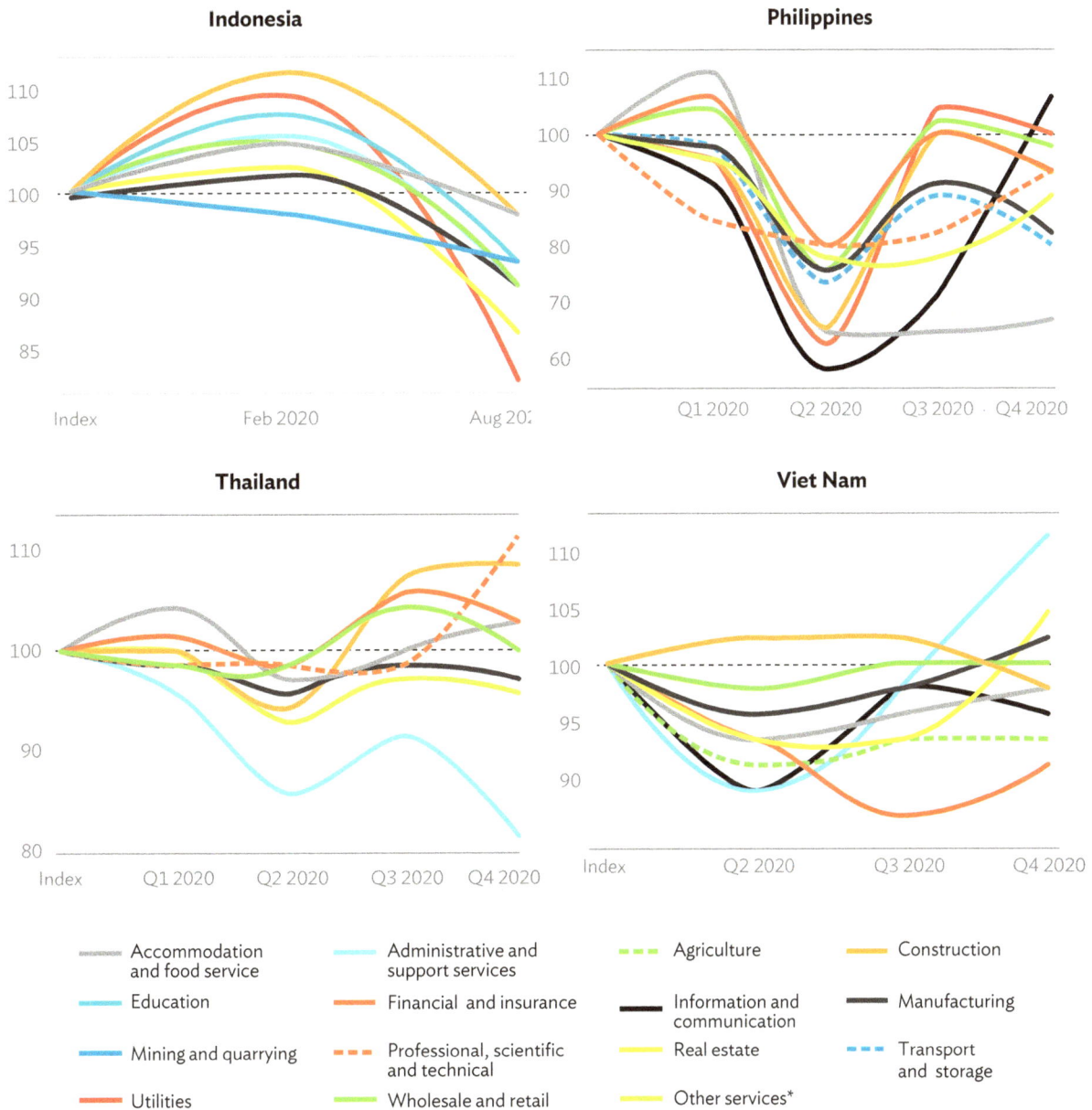

Indonesia

Philippines

Thailand

Viet Nam

Legend:
- Accommodation and food service
- Administrative and support services
- Agriculture
- Construction
- Education
- Financial and insurance
- Information and communication
- Manufacturing
- Mining and quarrying
- Professional, scientific and technical
- Real estate
- Transport and storage
- Utilities
- Wholesale and retail
- Other services*

Employment index, corresponding quarter of 2019 = 100, to control for seasonality.
*Other services includes the following ISIC Rev 4. categories: R. Arts, entertainment and recreation, S. Other service Activities, T. Activities of households as employers; undifferentiated goods- and services- producing activities of households for own use; U. Activities of extraterritorial organizations and bodies.
Source: Labor force surveys of various countries.

In sum, although the second half of 2020 saw a rebound in employment in the sample countries, job gains consisted primarily of own-account and unpaid family work and informal employment. Labor reallocation toward lower productivity sectors showed that these sectors absorbed some of the workers who were displaced in Q2 (labor market reentrants) in addition to new entrants who may have otherwise had more productive employment opportunities.

Intensive Margins of Adjustment: Working-Hour Reductions

The previous sections discussed the extensive margins of labor market adjustment to the COVID-19 shock, specifically employment losses resulting in shifts across labor force status, and labor reallocation or shifts within employment. Job losses underestimate the employment impact of the pandemic, however, due to significant reductions in working time. Specifically, those still employed worked less hours or no hours at all, as firms limited operations and resorted to intensive margins of adjustment to preserve employment relationships, and as self-employed workers abided by curfews, lockdowns, and other constraints on their activities. For this reason, the International Labour Organization (ILO) used the decline in working hours as a key indicator to monitor the COVID-19 crisis' impact on labor markets. Following the approach used in the ILO Monitor series (ILO 2020a, 2020b),[11] this report provides a decomposition of working-hour losses to assess the extent of intensive and extensive margins of adjustment used at different stages of the crisis (see Appendix A1 for the methodology). In this context, the intensive margins refer specifically to working-hour reductions while remaining employed, while extensive margins refer to job losses.

In the Philippines, intensive margins of adjustment accounted for the majority of working-hour losses in Q2 2020 in all sectors except in utilities and public administration (Table 1.3). In Indonesia as well, extensive margins dominated in these two sectors, as well as in agriculture, construction, finance and real estate, and human health and social services. In Thailand and Viet Nam, in several sectors—including agriculture, manufacturing, information and communication, real estate, professional, scientific and technical activities, administrative and support services, and education—firms were more likely to resort to extensive margins. But aggregate-level and broad sector-level trends hide significant heterogeneity across industries. At a more disaggregated level (2-digit International Standard Industrial Classification [ISIC]), intensive margins of adjustment accounted for the majority of Q2 2020 working-hour losses in 70% industries in the Philippines, approximately half of industries in Thailand, and one quarter in Viet Nam.[12] In all three countries with available LFS microdata for Q3 2020 (in the Philippines, Thailand, and Viet Nam), a rebound in working hours resulted mainly from the increased working hours of those still employed. Working hours recovered in many sectors but remained well below the prepandemic levels.

---

[11]   The ILO Monitor series presents and provides updates of regional and global estimates of labor market adjustments in terms of workplace closures, reductions in working-hour losses, and labor income losses.

[12]   Based on authors' calculations from LFS. This statistic could not be computed for Indonesia due to the lack of detailed data on economic activity in the LFS. At a less disaggregated level (1-digit ISIC), the intensive margins represented the larger part of working-hour losses in approximately 60% of industries.

Table 1.3: Decomposition of Working-Hour Losses – Intensive Margins of Adjustment, Q2 2020

(%)

	Indonesia*	Philippines	Viet Nam	Thailand
Agriculture	37.1	65.3	0	0
Mining and quarrying	100.0	63.9	100	0
Manufacturing	51.6	65.4	0	0
Utilities	24.9	47.0	100	0
Construction	31.6	64.2	91	57.2
Wholesale and retail	84.4	55.2	66	69.0
Transport and storage	93.7	72.3	71	78.8
Accommodation and food service	100.0	55.8	69	81.2
Information and communication	50.5	59.9	0	0
Financial and insurance	0.0	58.4	0	0
Real estate	27.5	68.7	0	0
Professional, scientific and technical	60.6	79.9	0	16.8
Administrative and support service	80.6	80.4	24	47.2
Public administration	22.1	36.9	98	85.2
Education	54.4	80.3	0	77.2
Human health and social work	24.0	54.2	100	30.3
Other services	100.0	58.6	78	67.7

* For Indonesia, working-hour decline refers to the period from February to August 2020.
Notes: Intensive margins are calculated as per Appendix A1. Negative values are set to zero, values greater than 100% are set to 100.
Source: Authors' calculations based on labor force surveys of various countries.

Several factors may have influenced the adjustment patterns or the relative importance of intensive versus extensive adjustment to the COVID-19 shock across countries and industries. For instance, the possibility of working from home, at least partially, may have helped limit job losses, and other factors (such as wage and salaried workers share firm size distribution, wage subsidies, and other policy incentives, among others) may have played a role in determining adjustment patterns at the sectoral level. While data required for a thorough analysis of these issues are not yet available, this report tentatively explores some of these potential factors based on insights from the LFS. Specifically, for the countries with available quarterly LFS microdata, we examined the correlation between some of these factors and the intensive margin of adjustment in Q2 2020 at the 2-digit ISIC level.[13]

We employ the "teleworkability" indices of occupations (Generalao 2021), which represent the degree to which tasks involved in an occupation can be effectively done from home or offsite, to assess whether the share of "teleworkable occupations" could be a determining factor in the use of intensive margins of adjustment at the sectoral level. In the Philippines, the sectors in which intensive margins accounted for the highest shares of adjustment included those with large shares of teleworkable occupations (e.g., education, professional, scientific and technical activities, administration and support services, and real estate), while some sectors with relatively low teleworkability indices were less likely to resort to intensive margins (utilities, accommodation and restaurants, wholesale and retail trade) (Table 1.3). However, intensive margins were also widely used in sectors like agriculture, manufacturing, mining, construction, transportation and storage, and other services.

---

[13] Please refer to Table A1.2 for a description of the correlation analysis and the resulting correlation matrix.

Overall, there appears to be no significant correlation between the teleworkability of occupations and the degree to which intensive margins were used in all three countries with available data. We also did not find any statistically significant correlation at the sectoral level between the use of intensive adjustment margins and (i) wage and salaried employment as a share of sectoral employment; (ii) micro, small, and medium-sized enterprises (MSMEs) share in sectoral employment; and (iii) low-skilled workers share in sectoral employment. The correlation coefficient for the temporary workers share in wage employment (in the Philippines) is statistically significant, suggesting a strong negative association with the use of intensive margins of adjustment. This supports the idea that temporary workers are more easily "let go" in times of crisis and are therefore more vulnerable (see Chapter 2). Moreover, teleworkability has a statistically significant positive association with wage and salaried work, and negative association with the share of low-skill workers and temporary workers in across countries with available data. This indicates that employees , particularly those with permanent working arrangements are more likely to shift to telework than their self-employed, lower skilled and temporary employee counterparts.

Another factor that can potentially determine the relative use of intensive and extensive margins of adjustment is policy, specifically the implementation of labor market measures aimed at limiting job losses. As further discussed in Chapter 3, all five sample countries implemented job protection policies including some kind of wage subsidies in the course of 2020, and some (the Philippines and Viet Nam) also provided incentives for employers to shift to flexible work arrangements and avoid layoffs. Policies differed across countries in terms of their focus, coverage, targeting, and timing of implementation, among other things. In Indonesia, wage subsidies were implemented at the end of August and would therefore not have been effective in the period covered here. The other three countries began implementing job protection policies/wage subsidies earlier by the end of March 2020 for the Philippines, and in April 2020 for Thailand and Viet Nam.

Chapter 2

Differential Impacts
of the Pandemic

2 Key Findings

Virtually all age and sex cohorts experienced a movement out of employment, either into unemployment or out of the labor force in Indonesia, Malaysia, the Philippines, Thailand, and Viet Nam in Q2 2020.

Young workers in Southeast Asia were severely impacted because they are overrepresented and disproportionately affected by job cuts in hard-hit sectors.

More women exited the labor force following job loss while more men transitioned to unemployment. This is partly because women take on a greater share of the care burden (including childcare and homeschooling, and caring for ill relatives).

Women who exited the labor force in Q2 2020 were quicker to reenter in Q3 2020 than men, partly owing to an "added-worker effect" in which additional workers join the labor force to compensate for the lost jobs and income of other household members.

Low-skilled workers (elementary occupations and agriculture workers) made up a large share of Q2 2020 job losses across the region, along with middle-skilled sales and service workers. Also hit hard across the region were middle-skilled workers in manufacturing and construction.

Throughout 2020, self-employment income was the most affected source of household income across the region.

Informal workers, temporary and casual workers, and migrant workers constituted particularly vulnerable groups.

The differential effects on firms resulted partly from the highly sectoral impacts of the crisis as well as the influence of characteristics like the firm's size and export orientation.

The recovery of employment in Q3 2020 depicted a shift toward "lower-quality" work.

Youth faced major labor market challenges BEFORE COVID-19

Youth unemployment rates soared at least **5 times as high** as adult rates across many countries in the region

In Indonesia and the Philippines, approximately **one out of four young women** were not in employment, education, or training

...and were hit hardest DURING the pandemic

Share of Youth in Job Losses

INO 22%

PHI 23%

THA 28%

VIE 45%

CLOSED

Youth accounted for **22%–45%** of total job losses in Q2 2020 in Indonesia, the Philippines, Thailand, and Viet Nam, while representing only **10%–15%** of total employment in these countries

Women in some sectors and occupational groups were disproportionately affected.

In Q2 2020:
In Thailand, women accounted for **91%** of job losses in manufacturing, and **58%** of job losses overall

In the Philippines, nearly **one out of four women** lost their jobs in sales and service occupations

The crisis had differential impacts across skills groups and occupations.

Distribution of job losses (average for Indonesia, the Philippines, Thailand, and Viet Nam) in Q2 2020

About 30% Low-skilled elementary occupations and agriculture workers

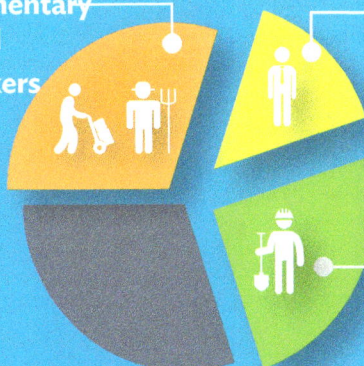

15% Middle-skilled sales and service occupations

25% Middle-skilled occupations in manufacturing (crafts and related trades, plant and machine operators, and assemblers)

In addition to high informality and working poverty mentioned in Chapter 1, there were major inequalities in Southeast Asia in terms of labor market outcomes across groups, along various dimensions—including age, gender, skills, and geographic location before the COVID-19 pandemic, which were not only exposed further but also exacerbated by the crisis. Chapter 2 examines the differential impacts of the crisis across demographic groups (section 2.1) and occupational and skill-level categories (section 2.2). Section 2.3 identifies various groups that were particularly vulnerable to the crisis because of the nature of their work, type of working arrangements, and other factors like migration status, while section 2.4 briefly discusses differential impacts across firms. The data presented in this chapter are based on quarterly labor force surveys (LFSs) conducted for Indonesia, Malaysia, the Philippines, Thailand, and Viet Nam.[1] Insights from the LFSs are supplemented with data obtained from two rounds of household surveys performed by the Asian Development Bank Institute (ADBI) in member countries of the Association of Southeast Asian Nations (ASEAN), which provide information on household income losses from various sources.[2]

Impact by Demographic Groups

Youth and Women in Southeast Asian Labor Markets

Before the pandemic, women and youth faced major labor market challenges in many parts of Southeast Asia, with high youth unemployment, an elevated share of youth not in employment, education, or training (NEET) across many countries, and widening gender gaps in labor market outcomes in some countries. Youth unemployment rates were at least 5 times as high as adult rates across countries. NEET rates were high across the region particularly among young women, such as in Indonesia and the Philippines where approximately one out of four young women was NEET in 2019 (Figure 2.1). Gender gaps in labor force participation rates (LFPRs) and the employment-to-population ratio (EPR) were most significant in Indonesia, Malaysia, and the Philippines, with men being 1.5 to 1.6 times as likely as women to participate in the labor market. Among the countries with available quarterly LFS data, Viet Nam had the lowest gender gap in labor force participation and, consequently, one of the highest overall LFPR and EPR among Southeast Asian countries.[3] In 2019, approximately three-quarters of the working-age population in Viet Nam and over two-thirds of the working-age population in Malaysia and Thailand was employed. Women and youth were also overrepresented among vulnerable groups, which included informal and low-skilled workers. Given their initial disadvantages in the region's labor markets, it is not surprising to see women and youth among the groups most vulnerable to the impact of the COVID-19 crisis.

---

[1]   The occupational group- and skill-level variable was available for all five countries. The Viet Nam LFS allowed us to distinguish between formal and informal employment. The variable for type of working arrangement is available in the LFS for the Philippines and for Viet Nam, and an enterprise size variable is included in the LFS for Thailand and for Viet Nam.

[2]   Two rounds of the surveys were conducted via telephone due to COVID-19 in these countries: Cambodia, Indonesia, the Lao People's Democratic Republic (Lao PDR), Malaysia, the Philippines, Thailand, and Viet Nam. For round one, data were collected from the end of May to the end of June 2020, and round two covered early July 2020 to the end of December 2020. The survey was designed by ADBI and implemented by five survey companies in these countries. The questionnaires include questions on the characteristics of households (e.g., number of members, gender, number employed, number in school, age of head of household, education level, urban versus rural residence, and income, including types of income) and changes in income, employment, and working hours compared with the base period at the end of 2019, among others (Morgan and Trinh 2021).

[3]   In 2019, other countries in the region with the highest LFPR were Cambodia (82.0%) and the Lao PDR (78.1%). Source: ILOSTAT database [Data Explorer]. https://ilostat.ilo.org/data/ (accessed 11 October 2021).

Figure 2.1: LFPR, EPR, Unemployment Rate, and NEET Rate by Demographic Group, 2019
(%)

EPR

	Indonesia	Malaysia	Philippines	Thailand	Viet Nam
Total	65.5	62.6	58.7	66.3	75.8
Male youth	48.1	44.4	41.4	45.5	55.7
Female youth	34.5	30.4	26.3	31.4	48.6
Male adults	88.6	84.1	83.5	80.8	86.4
Female adults	57.0	55.1	52.8	63.2	76.1

LFPR

	Indonesia	Malaysia	Philippines	Thailand	Viet Nam
Total	68.0	64.7	60.0	66.7	77.4
Male youth	55.6	49.8	44.0	47.1	59.6
Female youth	39.7	35.1	28.6	33.2	52.1
Male adults	90.3	85.7	84.6	81.1	87.6
Female adults	57.9	56.2	53.6	63.4	77.1

Unemployment Rate

	Indonesia	Malaysia	Philippines	Thailand	Viet Nam
Total	3.6	3.3	2.2	0.7	2.0
Male youth	13.6	10.7	5.8	3.4	6.6
Female youth	13.0	13.4	8.1	5.5	6.7
Male adults	1.9	1.8	1.3	0.4	1.3
Female adults	1.4	1.8	1.5	0.3	1.3

NEET Rate

	Indonesia	Malaysia	Philippines	Thailand	Viet Nam
Male youth	15.1	9.2	13.8	11.2	12.1
Female youth	26.1	16.3	24.1	18.6	17.4

EPR = employment-to-population ratio; LFPR = labor force participation rate; NEET = not in employment, education, or training.
Sources: Labor force surveys of various countries; International Labour Organization (ILO). ILOSTAT. https://ilostat.ilo.org/data/ (accessed 11 October 2021).

Transitions across Labor Force Statuses by Age and Sex Cohorts

Using pseudo panels constructed by sex and age cohorts (5-year bands) to follow the progression of demographic groups across labor force statuses (transitions from employment to unemployment, exits from labor force), we find that across the sample countries, virtually all age and sex cohorts experienced a movement out of employment into unemployment and out of the labor force in the second quarter (Q2) of 2020, which represents the peak of labor market impacts of the crisis as explained in Chapter 1 (Figure 2.2).

Figure 2.2: Net Transitions across Labor Force Statuses by Age and Sex Cohort, Q2 2020

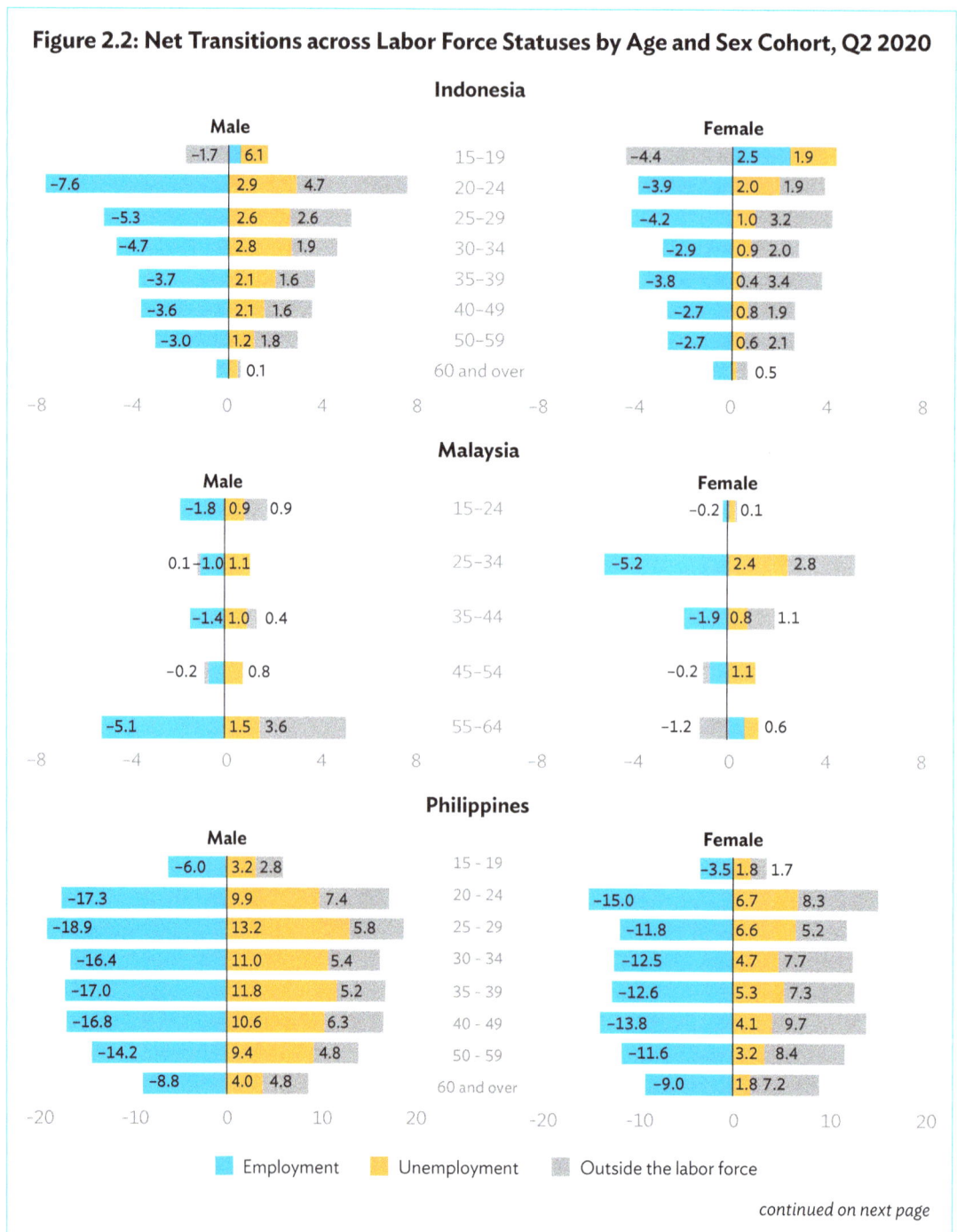

Indonesia

Male

Age	Employment	Unemployment	Outside the labor force
15–19	-1.7	6.1	
20–24	-7.6	2.9	4.7
25–29	-5.3	2.6	2.6
30–34	-4.7	2.8	1.9
35–39	-3.7	2.1	1.6
40–49	-3.6	2.1	1.6
50–59	-3.0	1.2	1.8
60 and over			0.1

Female

Age	Employment	Unemployment	Outside the labor force
15–19	-4.4	2.5	1.9
20–24	-3.9	2.0	1.9
25–29	-4.2	1.0	3.2
30–34	-2.9	0.9	2.0
35–39	-3.8	0.4	3.4
40–49	-2.7	0.8	1.9
50–59	-2.7	0.6	2.1
60 and over			0.5

Malaysia

Male

Age	Employment	Unemployment	Outside the labor force
15–24	-1.8	0.9	0.9
25–34	0.1	-1.0	1.1
35–44	-1.4	1.0	0.4
45–54	-0.2		0.8
55–64	-5.1	1.5	3.6

Female

Age	Employment	Unemployment	Outside the labor force
15–24	-0.2		0.1
25–34	-5.2	2.4	2.8
35–44	-1.9	0.8	1.1
45–54	-0.2		1.1
55–64	-1.2		0.6

Philippines

Male

Age	Employment	Unemployment	Outside the labor force
15 - 19	-6.0	3.2	2.8
20 - 24	-17.3	9.9	7.4
25 - 29	-18.9	13.2	5.8
30 - 34	-16.4	11.0	5.4
35 - 39	-17.0	11.8	5.2
40 - 49	-16.8	10.6	6.3
50 - 59	-14.2	9.4	4.8
60 and over	-8.8	4.0	4.8

Female

Age	Employment	Unemployment	Outside the labor force
15 - 19	-3.5	1.8	1.7
20 - 24	-15.0	6.7	8.3
25 - 29	-11.8	6.6	5.2
30 - 34	-12.5	4.7	7.7
35 - 39	-12.6	5.3	7.3
40 - 49	-13.8	4.1	9.7
50 - 59	-11.6	3.2	8.4
60 and over	-9.0	1.8	7.2

■ Employment   ■ Unemployment   ■ Outside the labor force

continued on next page

Figure 2.2 continued

Thailand

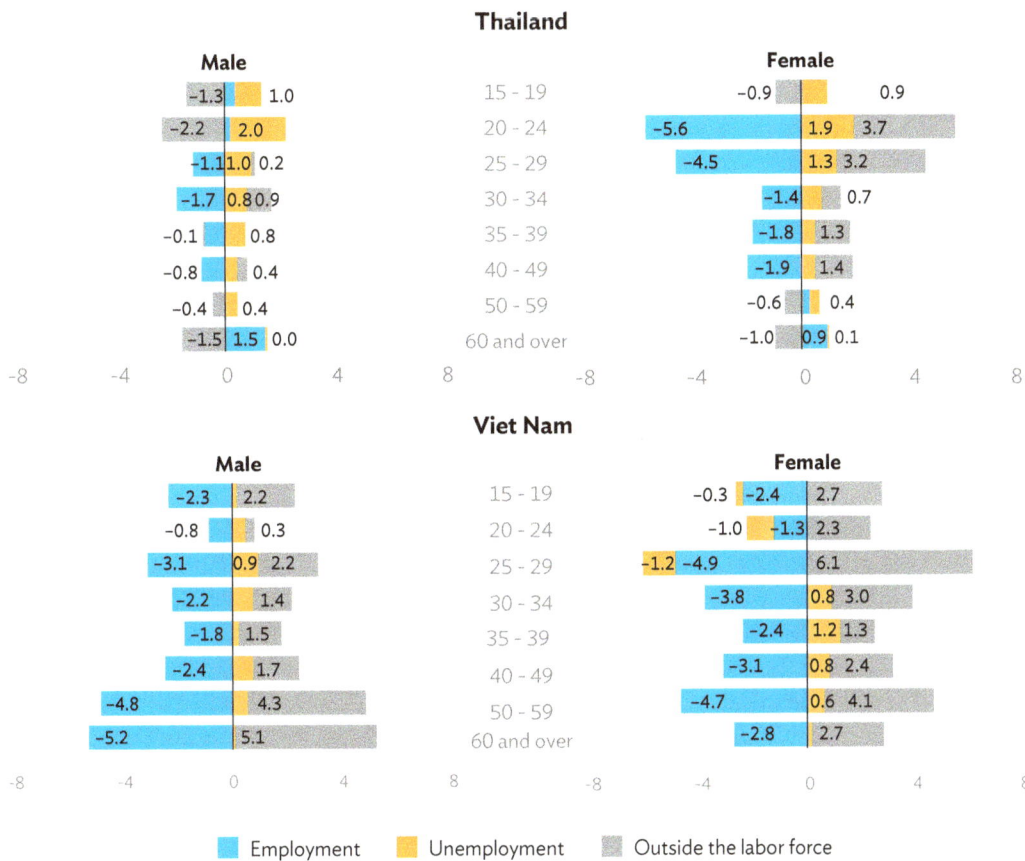

Male

-1.3	1.0	15 - 19
-2.2	2.0	20 - 24
-1.1 1.0 0.2		25 - 29
-1.7 0.8 0.9		30 - 34
-0.1	0.8	35 - 39
-0.8	0.4	40 - 49
-0.4	0.4	50 - 59
-1.5 1.5 0.0		60 and over

Female

-0.9	0.9	15 - 19
-5.6	1.9 3.7	20 - 24
-4.5	1.3 3.2	25 - 29
-1.4	0.7	30 - 34
-1.8	1.3	35 - 39
-1.9	1.4	40 - 49
-0.6	0.4	50 - 59
-1.0 0.9 0.1		60 and over

Viet Nam

Male

-2.3	2.2	15 - 19
-0.8	0.3	20 - 24
-3.1	0.9 2.2	25 - 29
-2.2	1.4	30 - 34
-1.8	1.5	35 - 39
-2.4	1.7	40 - 49
-4.8	4.3	50 - 59
-5.2	5.1	60 and over

Female

-0.3 -2.4	2.7	15 - 19
-1.0 -1.3	2.3	20 - 24
-1.2 -4.9	6.1	25 - 29
-3.8	0.8 3.0	30 - 34
-2.4	1.2 1.3	35 - 39
-3.1	0.8 2.4	40 - 49
-4.7	0.6 4.1	50 - 59
-2.8	2.7	60 and over

■ Employment   ■ Unemployment   ▨ Outside the labor force

Note: Data for Indonesia refer to the period March–August 2020.
Source: Authors' estimates based on labor force surveys of various countries.

In all countries of the region, youth represented a higher-than-average share of the workforce in hard-hit sectors. They were also disproportionately affected in terms of job cuts in these sectors (Figure 2.3), often as a consequence of having less experience and being less likely to have permanent contract arrangements, which make them the first to be let go during the crisis (ILO 2020e). For instance, youth (aged 15–24) accounted for 22%–28% of total job losses in Q2 2020 in Indonesia, Thailand, and the Philippines, while representing only 10%–15% of total employment in these countries in Q4 2019 (Figure 2.3). In Viet Nam, youth accounted for as much as 45% of job losses in Q2 2020, despite representing only 12% of total employment in Q4 2019.

Transitions into unemployment were more significant among youth cohorts than adult cohorts across all countries except Viet Nam (Figure 2.2). In the three youngest age cohorts in Viet Nam, net transitions from employment out of the labor force were accompanied by transitions from unemployment out of the labor force as well. As a result, the female youth unemployment rate actually declined in Q2 2020 in Viet Nam.

In some countries, the recovery of employment for youth also lagged behind that of adults. For instance, in Malaysia, the youth employment-to-population ratio (EPR) and labor force participation rate (LFPR) continued to decline in Q3 2020, while the corresponding rates increased for adults (Table A2.1). In Viet Nam, while the adult EPR and LFPR had partially recovered by Q4

2020, the youth EPR and LFPR continued to decline throughout 2020 and the first half of 2021. By Q2 2021, the youth EPR in Viet Nam stood at 39.9%, more than 12 percentage points below its precrisis (Q4 2019) level, and the youth unemployment rate had reached the highest point since the onset of the pandemic. In Thailand as well, youth continued to be heavily affected in Q1 2021, with the youth EPR declining by as much as 2.9 percentage points, compared with 1.1 percentage points for adults.

Figure 2.3: Share of Youth in Sectoral Employment and in Net Job Losses, Q2 2020
(%)

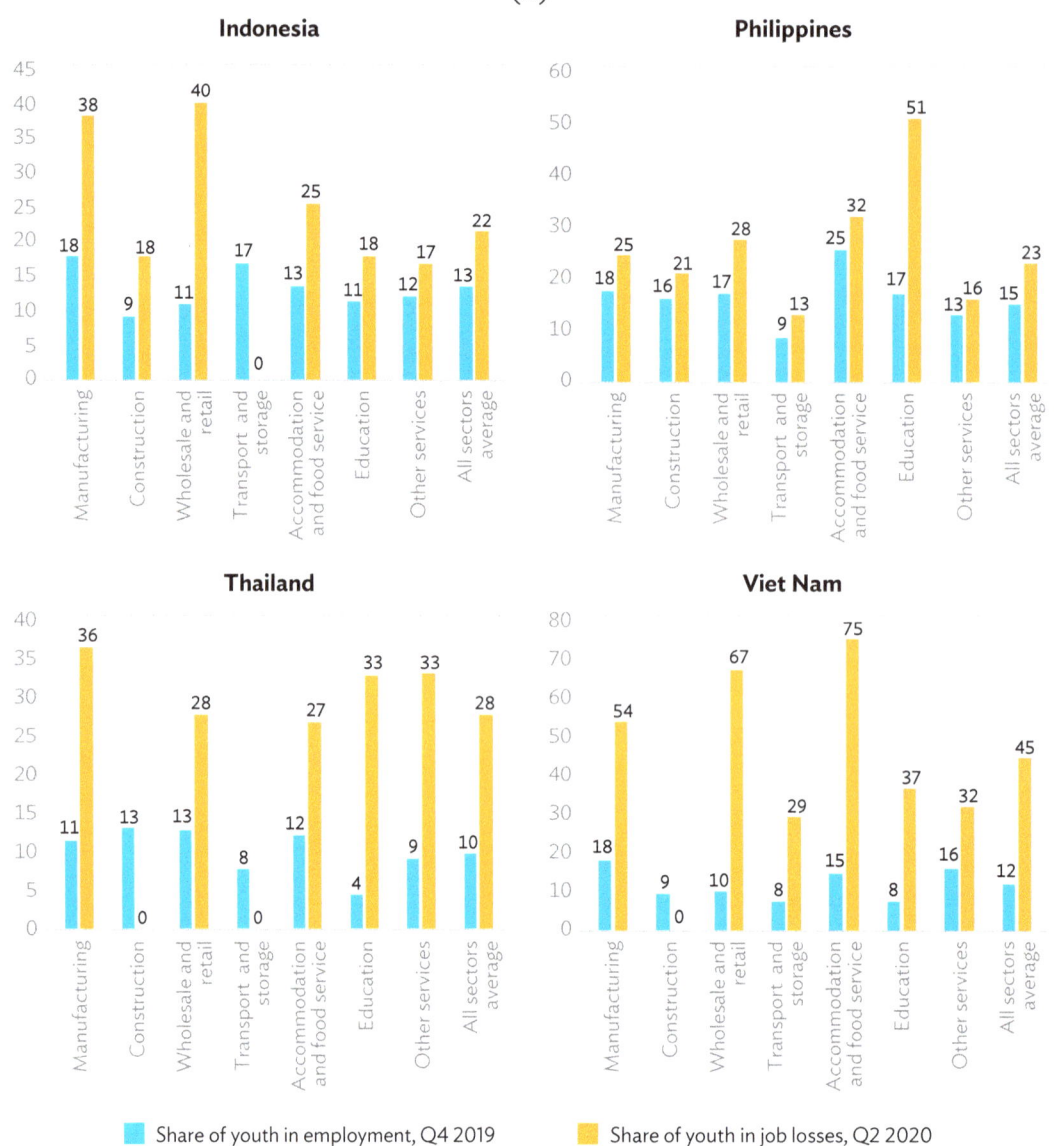

Indonesia

Sector	Share of youth in employment, Q4 2019	Share of youth in job losses, Q2 2020
Manufacturing	18	38
Construction	9	18
Wholesale and retail	11	40
Transport and storage	17	0
Accommodation and food service	13	25
Education	11	18
Other services	12	17
All sectors average	13	22

Philippines

Sector	Share of youth in employment, Q4 2019	Share of youth in job losses, Q2 2020
Manufacturing	18	25
Construction	16	21
Wholesale and retail	17	28
Transport and storage	9	13
Accommodation and food service	25	32
Education	17	51
Other services	13	16
All sectors average	15	23

Thailand

Sector	Share of youth in employment, Q4 2019	Share of youth in job losses, Q2 2020
Manufacturing	11	36
Construction	13	0
Wholesale and retail	13	28
Transport and storage	8	0
Accommodation and food service	12	27
Education	4	33
Other services	9	33
All sectors average	10	28

Viet Nam

Sector	Share of youth in employment, Q4 2019	Share of youth in job losses, Q2 2020
Manufacturing	18	54
Construction	9	0
Wholesale and retail	10	67
Transport and storage	8	29
Accommodation and food service	15	75
Education	8	37
Other services	16	32
All sectors average	12	45

■ Share of youth in employment, Q4 2019 ■ Share of youth in job losses, Q2 2020

Notes: Shares in employment refer to August 2019 for Indonesia and Q4 2019 for other countries. Youth shares in job losses refer to February–August 2020 for Indonesia and Q1–Q2 2020 for other countries.
Source: Authors' estimates based on labor force surveys of various countries.

In terms of the youth impacts of the pandemic, job losses among employed youth compounded disruptions in education and training. Additionally, for young labor market entrants and young workers hoping to move up the career ladder, the crisis may have substantially hampered these important transitions, with potential longer-term implications in terms of "scarring" (ILO 2020e).[4]

Women were disproportionately affected as well, recording a greater share in job losses than their share in employment. In Indonesia and the Philippines, where they represented 38%–39% of the workforce in Q4 2019, women accounted for 44% of job losses in Q2 2020 (Figure 2.4).

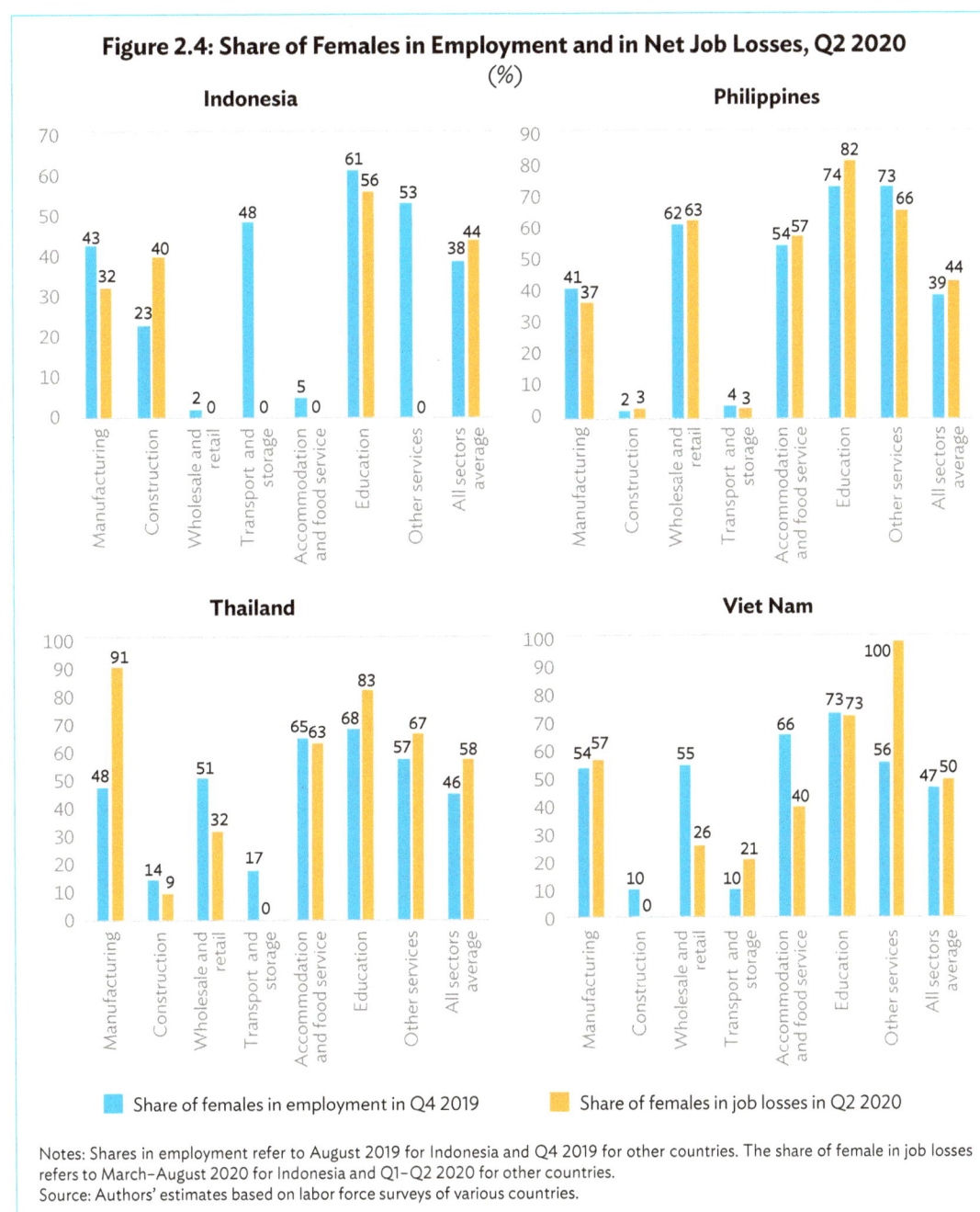

Figure 2.4: Share of Females in Employment and in Net Job Losses, Q2 2020
(%)

Notes: Shares in employment refer to August 2019 for Indonesia and Q4 2019 for other countries. The share of female in job losses refers to March–August 2020 for Indonesia and Q1–Q2 2020 for other countries.
Source: Authors' estimates based on labor force surveys of various countries.

---

[4] In particular, prolonged spells of unemployment early in a worker's career risk having longer-term impacts on their future employment and earning prospects.

In Viet Nam, they represented 47% of the workforce and accounted for half of the net job losses. In Thailand where they make up 47% of the workforce, women accounted for as much as 58% of job losses, in particular 91% of job losses in manufacturing. In Viet Nam, the share of females who lost their jobs was higher than the share of females employed in manufacturing, financial intermediation and insurance, administrative and support services, human health, and other service activities.[5] In the Philippines, the same was true in agriculture, accommodation and food services, administrative and support services, public administration, and education.

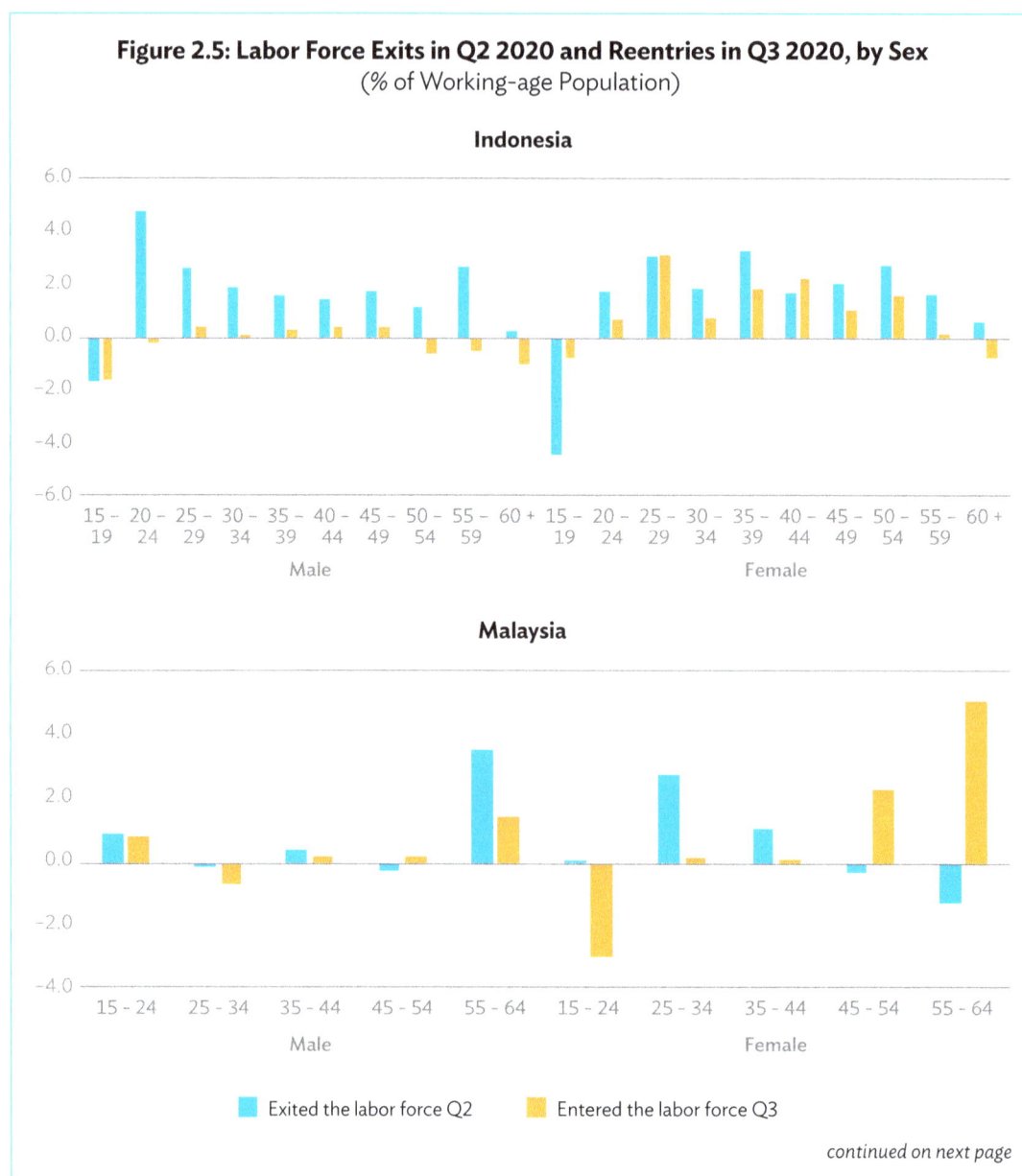

Figure 2.5: Labor Force Exits in Q2 2020 and Reentries in Q3 2020, by Sex
(% of Working-age Population)

Indonesia

Malaysia

■ Exited the labor force Q2   ■ Entered the labor force Q3

continued on next page

---

5   In Viet Nam, the manufacturing sector accounted for approximately 38% of net wage employment losses for women in Q2 2020 (compared with 28% for men).

Figure 2.5 continued

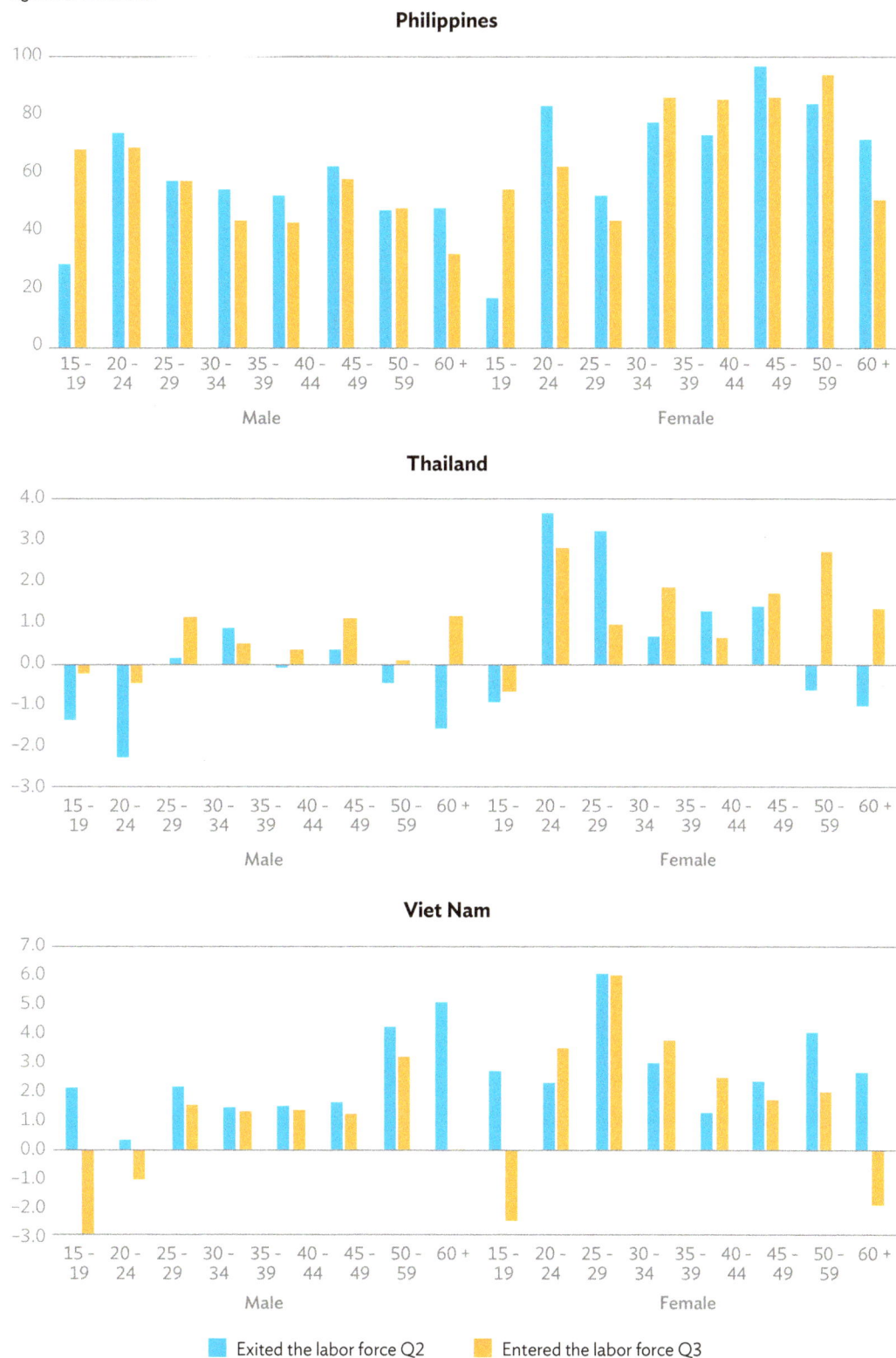

Philippines

Thailand

Viet Nam

Exited the labor force Q2   Entered the labor force Q3

Notes: The exits from the labor force period refer to March–August 2020 for Indonesia and Q1–Q2 2020 for other countries. The reentries into the labor force period correspond to September 2020–February 2021 for Indonesia and Q3–Q4 2020 for other countries.
Source: Authors' estimates based on labor force surveys of various countries.

One common feature of labor market adjustment to the COVID-19 shock across the sample countries is that more females moved into inactivity following job loss while more males moved into unemployment. The massive labor force exits among women are largely a consequence of their greater involvement in the care burden (such as childcare and homeschooling and caring for ill relatives), as has been observed across the world (ILO 2021a). This was true for all age cohorts in the Philippines and nearly all cohorts in the other countries (Figure 2.2). In countries where women are far less likely to participate in the labor market than men, greater labor market detachment among women can be particularly harmful if it lasts, as seemingly temporary disruptions to the working lives of women can have longer-lasting consequences.[6]

Is there evidence of greater detachment among women? Examining transitions in and out of the labor force for different age and sex cohorts in Q2 2020 revealed that, in general, women were indeed more likely than men to exit the labor force. However, these women were quicker to reenter the labor market in Q3 2020 than men. This may reflect a faster rebound of informal employment in comparison with formal wage employment (see section 2.3). Specifically, women who exited the labor force in Q2 2020 were more likely to reenter the labor market than men in Q3 2020 for all age cohorts in Indonesia, for 6 out of 8 cohorts in Thailand and Viet Nam, for 5 out of 8 cohorts (all cohorts over the age of 30) in the Philippines, and for 3 out of 5 cohorts in Malaysia (Figure 2.5). There also seems to be an "added-worker effect" in which additional women workers join the labor force to compensate for the lost jobs and income of other household members. These reentries into the labor force in Q3 were not only commensurate with, but actually surpassed, the women's exits in the previous quarter, as observed for many cohorts in Viet Nam, the Philippines, and Thailand. In Malaysia, the Philippines, and Thailand in particular, the Q3 2020 rebound in labor force participation rate was significant, particularly among adult women, bringing their LFPR back up above precrisis levels. The higher rebound in female labor force participation (relative to men) and the added-worker effect suggest that employment created during the recovery period could be of lower "quality" than employment lost due to the crisis. As of Q1 2021, the EPR and LFPR of adult women in Indonesia, Malaysia, the Philippines, and Thailand had surpassed their precrisis levels, while the corresponding rates for men remained well below their precrisis levels. In Viet Nam, both male and female EPRs and LFPRs had fallen back below their respective precrisis levels in Q2 2021.

Impact across Occupations and Skill Levels

The sectoral impacts of the pandemic and its disproportionate effect on jobs that require human interaction and involve tasks that cannot be carried out remotely are reflected in the occupational and skills distribution of job losses. In countries with available data, the occupational group comprising low-skilled worker categories[7]—elementary occupations and agriculture workers— accounted for the largest share in job losses in Q2 2020 (Figure 2.6).[8] Low-skilled workers represented nearly half of job losses in Viet Nam, and 25%–30% in Indonesia, Malaysia, the Philippines, and Thailand.

---

[6]   When a working-age person is not employed, they must be actively seeking and available to take up employment to be considered unemployed, as per the ILO definition. However, some persons may not be actively seeking employment although they are available to work, and others may be actively seeking work but not immediately available to work. The two latter categories of individuals are referred to as "potential labor force (PLF)" and are considered to have a stronger degree of labor market attachment, than other persons outside the labor force (Benes and Walsh 2018; De La Fuente 2011). Therefore, in this context, increased labor market detachment can be considered as a shift from unemployment or from the PLF to the category of persons who are neither seeking work nor available to work for various reasons.

[7]   Low-skilled workers include those in elementary occupations (International Standard Classification of Occupations [ISCO] code 9) and skilled agricultural, forestry and fishery workers (ISCO code 6).

[8]   For Indonesia, job losses refer to the period of March–August 2020.

Sales and service workers, a middle-skill occupational category, accounted for another quarter of job losses in the Philippines and more than 20% of job losses in Thailand, with an important impact on women. Female workers represented a large share (approximately 60% in Q1 2020) of this occupational workforce in these two countries and accounted for much of the decline in the occupational group's employment in Q2 2020 (73% in the Philippines and 62% in Thailand).[9]

Middle-skilled occupations in manufacturing and construction were also hit hard at this stage of the crisis, with plant and machine operators and craft and related trade workers representing 19%–26% of job losses in Q2 2020 in these countries (Figure 2.6). Women comprised over three-quarters of plant and machine operators job losses in Thailand, two-thirds of crafts and related trades workers job losses in Viet Nam in Q2 2020; but a minor share of job losses for these occupational groups in the Philippines and in Indonesia, where female employment in manufacturing is more limited.

Figure 2.6: Skills Level and Occupational Group Shares in Net Job Losses, Q2 2020
(%)

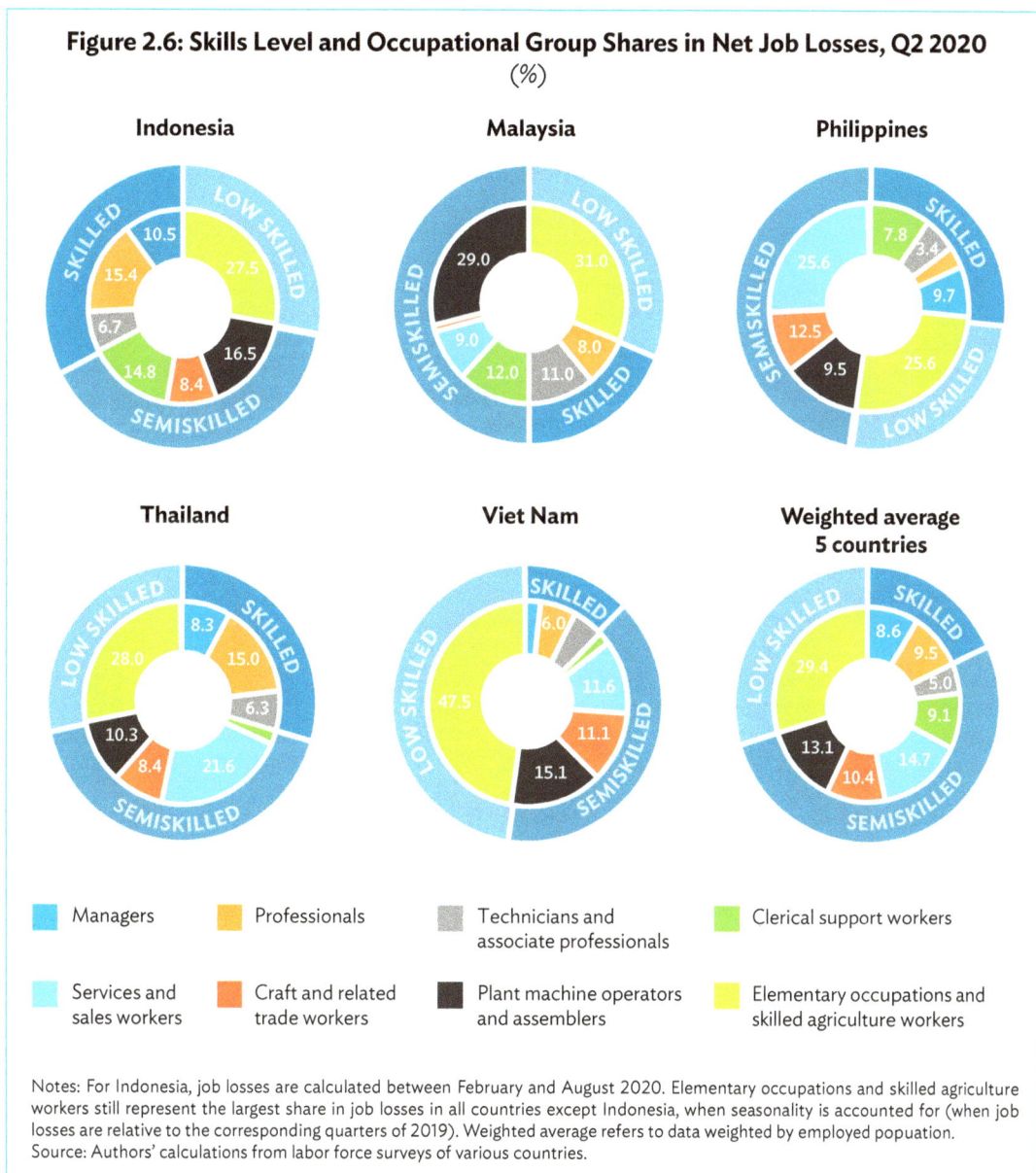

Indonesia — Skilled 10.5, 15.4; Low skilled 27.5; 6.7; 16.5; Semiskilled 14.8, 8.4

Malaysia — Low skilled 29.0, 31.0; 9.0; 12.0; 11.0; Skilled 8.0; Semiskilled

Philippines — Skilled 7.8, 3.4; 9.7; Semiskilled 25.6, 12.5, 9.5; Low skilled 25.6

Thailand — Low skilled 28.0; Skilled 8.3, 15.0; 6.3; 10.3; 8.4; Semiskilled 21.6

Viet Nam — Skilled 6.0; Low skilled 47.5; 11.6; 11.1; 15.1; Semiskilled

Weighted average 5 countries — Low skilled 29.4; Skilled 8.6, 9.5; 5.0; 9.1; 13.1; 10.4; 14.7; Semiskilled

Legend:
- Managers
- Professionals
- Technicians and associate professionals
- Clerical support workers
- Services and sales workers
- Craft and related trade workers
- Plant machine operators and assemblers
- Elementary occupations and skilled agriculture workers

Notes: For Indonesia, job losses are calculated between February and August 2020. Elementary occupations and skilled agriculture workers still represent the largest share in job losses in all countries except Indonesia, when seasonality is accounted for (when job losses are relative to the corresponding quarters of 2019). Weighted average refers to data weighted by employed popuation.
Source: Authors' calculations from labor force surveys of various countries.

[9] Authors' calculations based on labor force surveys.

As the economy reopened in the Philippines in Q3 2020, the low-skilled jobs created exceeded the number of low-skilled jobs lost in the previous quarter, reflecting the reallocation of labor toward these jobs. Low-skilled jobs accounted for almost half (47%–48%) of jobs recovered or created in the Philippines and in Viet Nam in Q3 2020. Similarly, in Thailand, low-skilled jobs—primarily in agriculture—accounted for most of the jobs created in Q3 2020, as manufacturing and construction continued to shed semiskilled jobs.

The COVID-19 crisis has therefore highlighted the significant vulnerability of low-skilled workers to external shocks and the continued countercyclical role played by low-skilled jobs (in agriculture and services) in absorbing displaced labor during crises. Moreover, some of the heavily affected jobs were those that could not be performed remotely, which includes many manufacturing jobs that are facing relatively high risk from automation in the region (see, for example, ADB 2021c). While this report focuses on short-term impacts, Box 2.1 discusses the potential longer-term implications for skills demand stemming from the COVID-19 crisis—particularly through the pandemic's interaction with technological change.

Box 2.1: Telework, Automation, and Digitalization – How COVID-19 Can Interact with Technology and Affect Jobs in Southeast Asia

Before the COVID-19 pandemic, technological change had already been contributing to increased inequality across and within countries in the Asia and Pacific region (ILO 2020i). The interaction of COVID-19 with technology may further expose and exacerbate inequalities across groups, based on skills, gender, and locality among other factors, through its impact on labor demand and supply. While the impact on labor supply also warrants consideration, this box focuses on the potential effects of the pandemic on labor demand trends. Specifically, discusses some of the channels through which the pandemic could have lasting impacts on labor and skills demand—through accelerating structural changes linked to automation, the shift to digital economy, and changing business processes and workplaces. Another channel through which the pandemic's interaction with technological change could have an impact on jobs in Southeast Asia is through restructuring of global supply chains (see Chapter 1, Box 1.1).

Whether COVID-19 has accelerated automation or the adoption of robots in Southeast Asia remains unclear. However, the region's countries have been consistently adding to their stock of industrial robots over the past decade (Müller et al. 2020). There is already some evidence that COVID-19 has triggered a lasting demand for digital adoption in the region—boosting growth in certain sectors of the internet economy and resulting in increased demand for medium- to high-level skills, such as technical and information and communication technology skills. The accelerated and continued growth in e-commerce, online media, and food delivery has offset contractions in transport and online travel. Overall, the internet economy is projected to grow by 24% to $309 billion in 2025 (Box Figure 2.1a), with important implications regarding the nature of jobs available in the near future.

While large shares of workers in advanced economies turned to remote work during periods of lockdown and confinement, the share of workers in "teleworkable" occupations was lower and differed across Southeast Asian economies. Teleworkability or the telework potential of jobs is an additional dimension through which technology may drive a wedge between high- and low-skilled workers (see literature on skill-biased technological change and routine-biased technological change, for instance, in ADB 2021c, as higher-skilled occupations tend to be more teleworkable or feasibly done from home or offsite. These occupations are also more likely to be located in developed and highly urbanized areas. For instance, in the Philippines, teleworkable occupations are concentrated in the National Capital Region (NCR), CALABARZON, and Central Luzon (Generalao 2021).

Box Figure 2.1b shows that the sectors hardest-hit by the COVID-19 crisis in the Philippines, such as construction, wholesale, and retail trade; repair of motor vehicles and motorcycles; transportation and storage; and accommodation and food service activities, are also those that are dominated by occupations with low telework potential.

continued on next page

Box 2.1 continued

Box Figure 2.1a: Internet Economy Gross Merchandise Value in Selected Southeast Asian Countries Overall and by Sector, CAGR

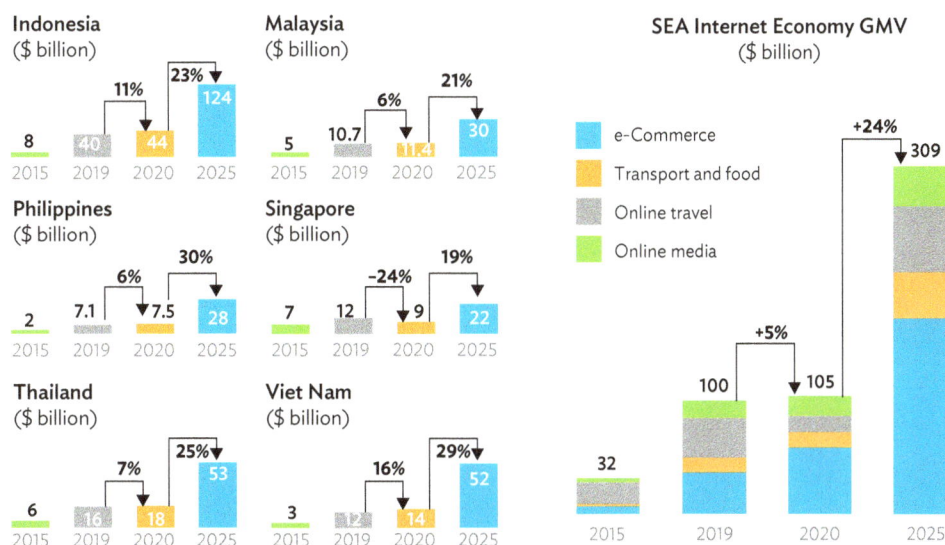

Indonesia
($ billion)

8 | 40 | 44 | 124
2015 | 2019 | 2020 | 2025
11% | 23%

Malaysia
($ billion)

5 | 10.7 | 11.4 | 30
2015 | 2019 | 2020 | 2025
6% | 21%

SEA Internet Economy GMV
($ billion)

- e-Commerce
- Transport and food
- Online travel
- Online media

32 | 100 | 105 | 309
2015 | 2019 | 2020 | 2025
+5% | +24%

Philippines
($ billion)

2 | 7.1 | 7.5 | 28
2015 | 2019 | 2020 | 2025
6% | 30%

Singapore
($ billion)

7 | 12 | 9 | 22
2015 | 2019 | 2020 | 2025
−24% | 19%

Thailand
($ billion)

6 | 16 | 18 | 53
2015 | 2019 | 2020 | 2025
7% | 25%

Viet Nam
($ billion)

3 | 12 | 14 | 52
2015 | 2019 | 2020 | 2025
16% | 29%

CAGR = compound annual growthrate, GMV = gross merchandise value, SEA = Southeast Asia.
Source: Google, Temasek, and Bain (2020).

Box Figure 2.1b: Weighted Average Teleworkability of Occupations by Major Industry Group in the Philippines, 2018 (%)

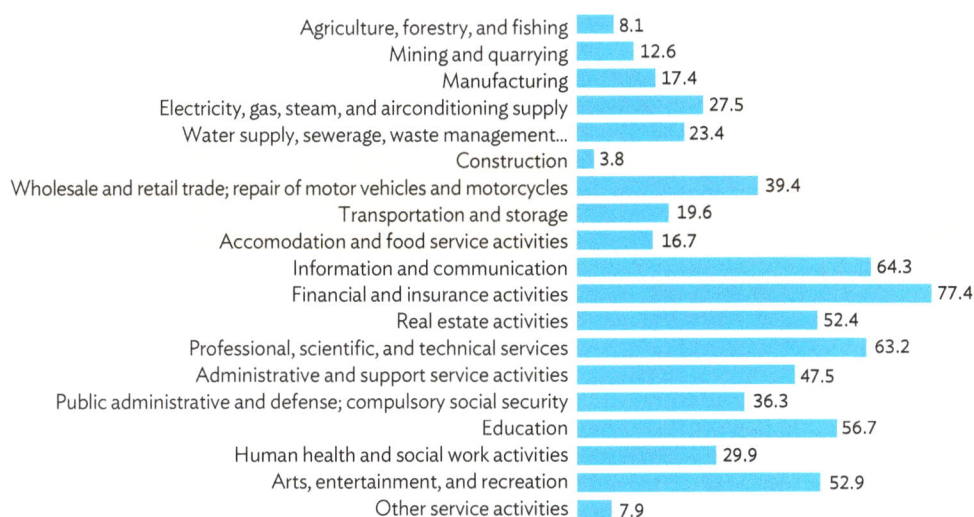

Industry Group	Value
Agriculture, forestry, and fishing	8.1
Mining and quarrying	12.6
Manufacturing	17.4
Electricity, gas, steam, and airconditioning supply	27.5
Water supply, sewerage, waste management...	23.4
Construction	3.8
Wholesale and retail trade; repair of motor vehicles and motorcycles	39.4
Transportation and storage	19.6
Accomodation and food service activities	16.7
Information and communication	64.3
Financial and insurance activities	77.4
Real estate activities	52.4
Professional, scientific, and technical services	63.2
Administrative and support service activities	47.5
Public administrative and defense; compulsory social security	36.3
Education	56.7
Human health and social work activities	29.9
Arts, entertainment, and recreation	52.9
Other service activities	7.9

Notes: Teleworkability refers to the degree to which a job can be feasibly done at home or offsite. The indices are derived by employing a task-based approach and classifying occupations based on whether the tasks involved are considered manual, require physically assisting and caring for others or must be done outdoors, and whether they can be effectively done with the aid of information and communication technology services and devices.
Source: Generalao (2021).

Sources: Generalao (2021); Google, Temasek, and Bain (2020); Müller et al. (2020).

Low-skilled workers represented nearly half of job losses in Viet Nam, and over a quarter in the Philippines and Thailand in Q2 2020

84%

Of surveyed households, 84% reported significant income losses from household business or own-account work in February–March 2020 and 58% in July–December 2020

62%

Informal workers made up 62% of job losses in Q2 2020 in Viet Nam

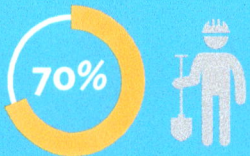

70%

Temporary workers and casual laborers represented approximately 70% of job losses in Q2 2020 in the Philippines

+70%

MSMEs accounted for over 70% of job losses in Thailand and Viet Nam in Q2 2020

Impacts on Various Groups of Workers

Beyond demographics and skill levels, the pandemic had differential effects on groups of workers based on their status in employment, the formality and nature of their contractual relationships and work arrangements, and their migration status, among others.

Labor reallocation across status-in-employment categories, specifically, toward own-account work in the second half of 2020, somewhat conceals the fact that own-account workers have been disproportionately affected by the pandemic across Southeast Asia. While close to 60% of households across the seven countries (Cambodia, Indonesia, the Lao People's Democratic Republic [Lao PDR], Malaysia, the Philippines, Thailand, and Viet Nam) included in both rounds of ADBI's household surveys in ASEAN countries reported a decline in income from wages and salaries, agriculture, and remittances, and as many as 84% of households reported income losses from self-employment (household business or own-account work) in the first period of February–March 2020 compared with the same period in 2019 (Figure 2.7). This source of income continued to be the most affected in the second period, with 58% of households reporting declines in income from this source between July and December 2020, compared with 46% from agriculture, 36% from remittances, and 35% from wages and salaries.

Informal workers make up another group that has been heavily affected by the COVID-19 crisis. This category includes many own-account workers, but also employees of enterprises in the informal and formal sectors. As mentioned, informal workers suffered major job losses (such as, for example, 62% of job losses in Q2 2020 in Viet Nam) and working time reductions given that many of them worked in heavily affected sectors. Informal workers are overrepresented among the region's working poor and near poor and limited access to social protection make them particularly vulnerable. Recognizing this, countries in the region have focused on expanding social assistance coverage, with some countries targeting informal workers in their response (see Chapter 3).

The informal workers category also intersects with workers in nonstandard forms of employment, including temporary workers and casual day laborers who have little job security and limited social protection coverage, due to the nature of their contractual arrangements. Temporary workers accounted for 61% of job losses in Viet Nam in Q2 2020, and workers in nonstandard forms of employment comprise some 70% of job losses in Q2 2020 in the Philippines. While informal workers and temporary workers accounted for the majority of job losses in Q2 2020, these workers were also the first to rebound in Q3 2020. In Viet Nam, for instance, informal employment and temporary employment accounted, respectively, for 89% and virtually all (100%) of net job creation (recovery) in Q3 2020 as

Figure 2.7: Share of Households in Selected Countries Reporting Decline in Income, by Income Source
(%)

Period 1: February – April 2020 versus February – April 2019

	All	Cambodia	Indonesia	Lao PDR	Malaysia	Philippines	Thailand	Viet Nam
Household business or self-business	83.6	86.7	86.6	76.5	69.4	88.1	89.5	81.0
Wages and salaries	59.9	62.2	69.0	31.0	46.5	81.0	61.2	64.3
Agriculture	58.0	28.7	81.4	66.3	54.3	76.4	70.8	58.5
Remittances	57.8	55.6	68.8	50.0	40.0	77.5	47.0	38.5

Period 2: December 2020 versus July 2020

	All	Cambodia	Indonesia	Lao PDR	Malaysia	Philippines	Thailand	Viet Nam
Household business or self-business	58.4	72.1	63.9	43.4	52.7	67.8	53.7	50.0
Agriculture	45.5	70.5	57.3	38.6	37.2	63.6	33.6	38.9
Remittances	36.0	45.0	30.9	65.5	15.2	44.9	15.6	39.3
Wages and salaries	35.2	47.7	33.8	20.4	28.8	49.2	32.3	35.2

Lao PDR = Lao People's Democratic Republic.
Notes: The decline in income in Period 1 relates to February-April 2020 versus the corresponding period in 2019. In Period 2, it relates to December 2020 versus July 2020.
Source: Authors' calculations using ADBI household survey data.

permanent jobs continued to decline (in net terms). These figures highlight the significant overlap between informal work and temporary work in some countries in the region.[10]

Migrant workers in general have been identified as a group that was severely hit by the pandemic (ILO 2020e). As international borders closed, many of these workers were stranded in either their home or host countries, often with no access to social protection or adequate health care. Migrant workers in Southeast Asia—often intraregional migrants—as well as international migrant workers originating from the region were no exception (see Box 2.2). A number of countries have targeted policies to address protection gaps for them (see Chapter 3).

---

[10]   Note that temporary workers are often not covered by social insurance and do not have benefits such as paid sick days, and are therefore by definition considered informal.

Box 2.2: COVID-19 Temporarily Halts Intraregional Migration—
Labor Migrants Hit Hard

Southeast Asia has always been defined by the significant movements of its population and as an important destination and source of labor migrants. The number of international migrants in the region has grown from around 2.9 million in 1990 to 10.6 million in 2020.[a] Most labor migrants in the region are in Malaysia and Thailand, accounting for about 10.7% and 5.7% of each country's population, respectively. About two-thirds of migrants come from countries within the region, i.e., 7.1 million intraregional migrants. Moreover, 3 of Asia's 20 biggest migration corridors are intraregional: Indonesia to Malaysia; Malaysia to Singapore; and the Lao People's Democratic Republic (Lao PDR) to Thailand (UNESCAP 2020). The region is also an important source of labor migrants at the global level. [a] With over 6 million emigrants, the Philippines is the top country of origin of overseas workers in the region, followed by Indonesia with 4.6 million emigrants.[a]

The COVID-19 pandemic struck migrant workers hard. Measures to control the pandemic, such as visa issuance restrictions, suspension of deployment, border closures, and shutdown of economic activities, caused migration to drop dramatically, effectively halting the typically bustling migration corridors in the region (ADBI, OECD, and ILO 2021). For example, Malaysia stopped allowing foreign nationals in March 2020. Although eventually easing employment pass categories I–III and professional visit pass restrictions, the admission of less-skilled workers with temporary employment passes remained suspended (ADBI, OECD, and ILO 2021). In addition, work permit registration for foreigners in Thailand declined to about one-third of prepandemic levels starting in April 2020 (Box Figure 2.2a). Furthermore, countries of the region saw a sharp decline in the number of outgoing workers (Box Figure 2.2b).

Box Figure 2.2a: Decline in Labor Migration Inflows to Destination Economies in Southeast Asia
('000)

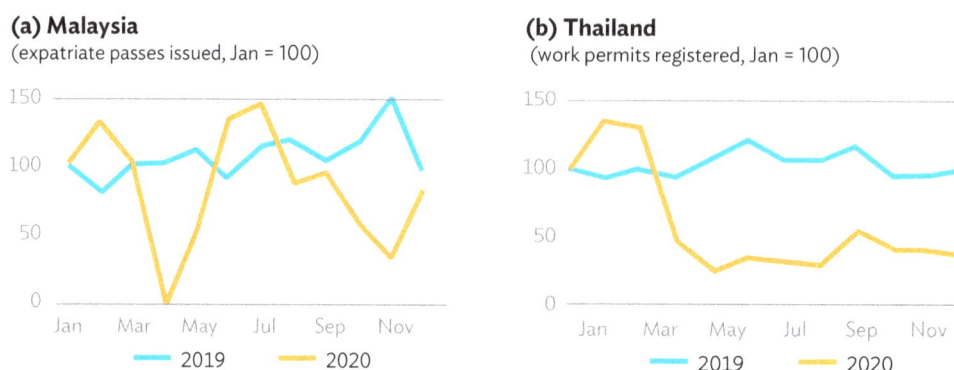

(a) Malaysia
(expatriate passes issued, Jan = 100)

(b) Thailand
(work permits registered, Jan = 100)

Source: ADBI, OECD, and ILO (2021).

While migrant workers historically supported different economic activities in their host countries, the pandemic exposed their poor living and working conditions, heightened vulnerability to job loss, and migration status affecting access to social protection. As countries in the region reeled from the unprecedented impacts of the pandemic on labor markets, migrant workers were among the first to lose their jobs. Most migrants predominantly work on fixed-term and temporary employment contracts, making them more vulnerable to job loss (ADBI, OECD, and ILO 2021).

continued on next page

Box 2.2 continued

Box Figure 2.2b: Changes in Outgoing Deployment, 2019–2020
(Jan = 100)

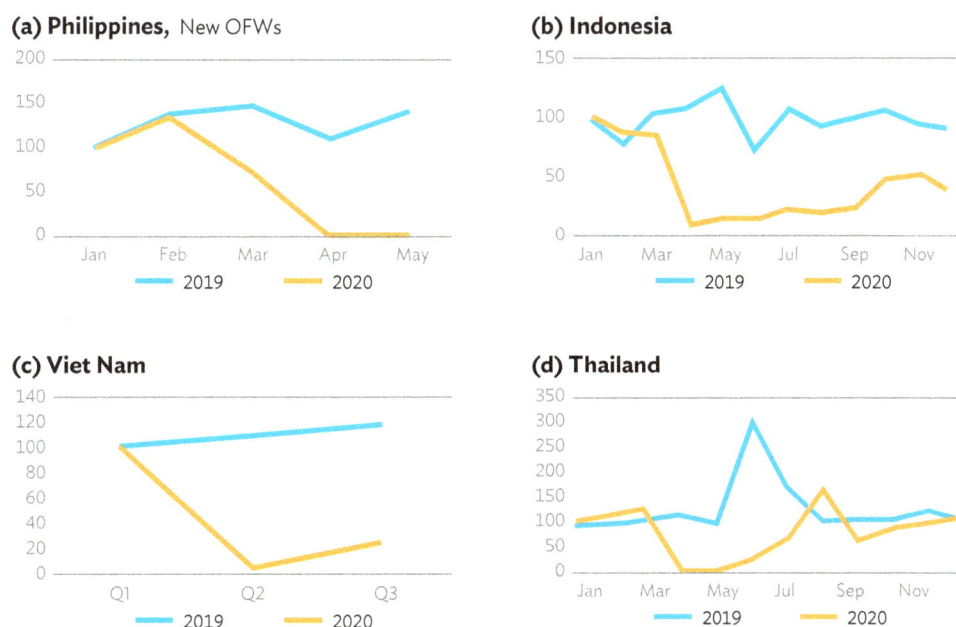

(a) Philippines, New OFWs

(b) Indonesia

(c) Viet Nam

(d) Thailand

OFW = overseas Filipino worker.
Source: ADBI, OECD, and ILO (2021).

Aggravating the precarious conditions of migrant workers was the lack of clarity on whether they could access health and welfare systems in their host countries (Srinivas and Sivaraman 2020 as cited in the Global Forum on Migration and Development COVID-19 Information Hub).[b] According to a rapid assessment survey performed by the International Labour Organization (ILO) on the impacts of COVID-19 on ASEAN migrant workers, 97% of respondents in destination countries had not accessed any social security support (ILO 2020g). As governments started introducing social protection measures to mitigate the impact of the pandemic, migrant workers were generally excluded from COVID-19 policy responses such as wage subsidies, unemployment benefits, or social security and social protection measures (ILO 2020f).

However, some Southeast Asian countries implemented policies to ensure migrant workers' welfare and reduce labor shortages due to border closures. In Thailand, for example, migrant workers in the formal sector who contributed to social security were entitled to unemployment benefits and severance pay (ILO 2020h). The Thailand government also provided special amnesty to more than 650,000 illegal migrant workers from other Southeast Asian countries (Charoensuthipan 2021). Under this program, illegal migrants who registered were allowed to legally stay and work in the country until 13 February 2023 without any penalties. Work permits were also extended for migrant workers with expiring visas in Thailand and Singapore (ILO 2021e). In Malaysia, foreign workers with work permits expiring in April through December 2020 were offered a 25% reduction in levy payments (ILO 2021e). In the Philippines displaced overseas Filipino workers (OFWs) were provided a one-time cash assistance of ₱10,000, which around 536,764 OFWs received as of July 2021 (Patinio 2021).

[a] United Nations Population Division. International Migrant Stock 2020 database. https://www.un.org/development/desa/pd/content/international-migrant-stock (accessed 27 October 2021).
[b] Global Forum on Migration and Development. COVID-19 Information Hub. Geneva. https://www.gfmd.org/covid-19 (accessed January 2020).
Sources: ADBI, OECD, and ILO (2021); ILO (2020f); (2020g); (2020h); (2021e).

Impacts across Firms

The pandemic also had differential impacts on firms, based on their size, export orientation, and access to finance and government support, among other factors. At the height of the pandemic in Q2 2020, micro, small, and medium-sized enterprises (MSMEs) were disproportionately affected, partly due to their being overrepresented in heavily hit sectors. In Thailand and Viet Nam, the two countries for which quarterly LFS data include a firm size variable, MSMEs accounted for 71% and 77% of job losses in Q2 2020, respectively.[11] This was in part due to the large employment shares of MSMEs in agriculture, wholesale and retail trade, transportation and storage, and accommodation and food services in these countries.

In the manufacturing sector, however, large firms—defined here as enterprises with over 50 employees—represented 65% of net job losses in Q2 2020 in Viet Nam and 71% in Thailand.[12] Larger manufacturing firms are more likely to be export oriented, and therefore heavily affected by supply chain shortages as well as declines in global demand (see Chapter 1, Box 1.1). In Thailand, in particular, employment in large enterprises in manufacturing continued to decline through Q4 2020 (Figure 2.8).

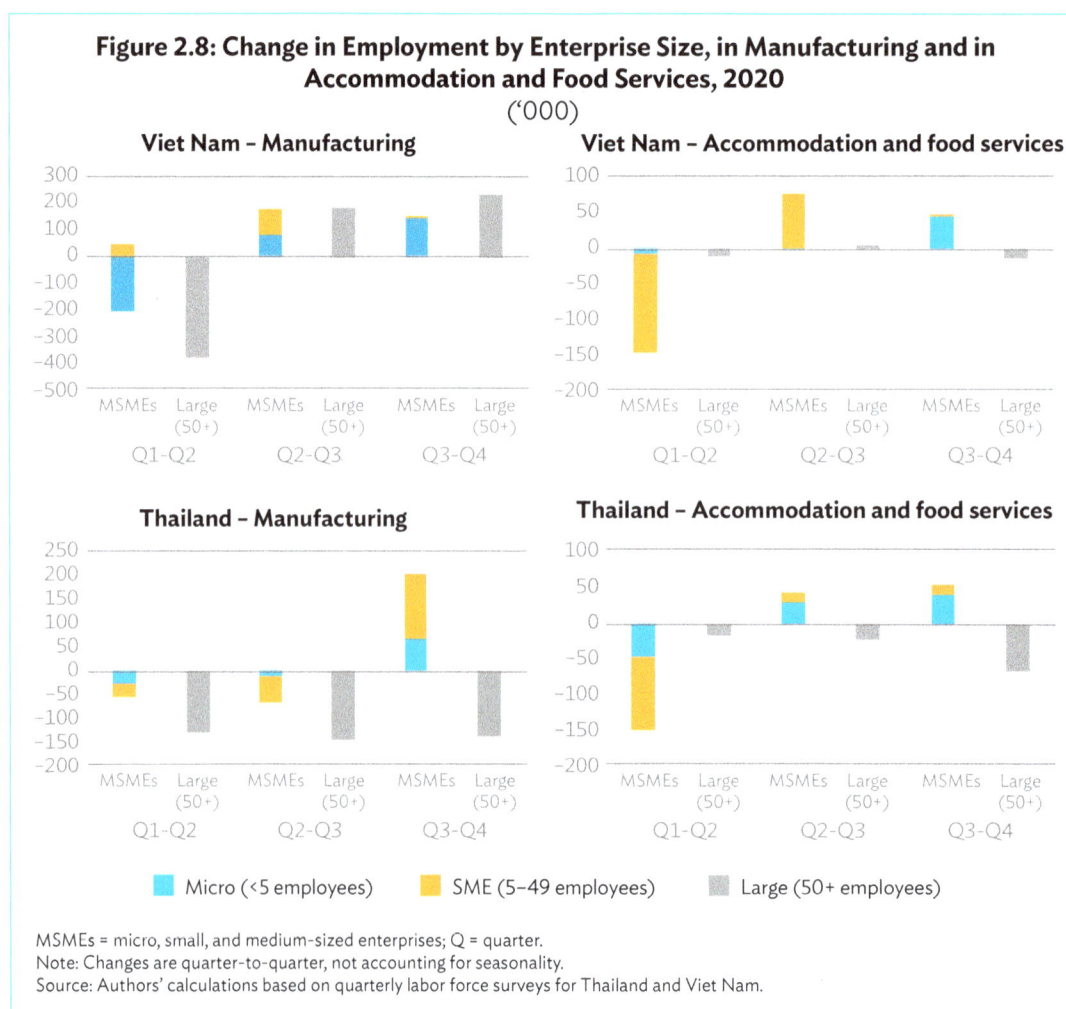

Figure 2.8: Change in Employment by Enterprise Size, in Manufacturing and in Accommodation and Food Services, 2020

('000)

MSMEs = micro, small, and medium-sized enterprises; Q = quarter.
Note: Changes are quarter-to-quarter, not accounting for seasonality.
Source: Authors' calculations based on quarterly labor force surveys for Thailand and Viet Nam.

---

[11]   Authors' calculations based on labor force surveys.

[12]   Authors' calculations based on labor force surveys.

Similarly, in the accommodation and food services sector, larger enterprises—although less affected by the crisis than MSMEs in the early stages—continued to shed jobs throughout 2020. In this sector as well, which is often used as a proxy for the tourism sector (see, for example, UNWTO 2020), larger enterprises rely more on international demand, which remained depressed throughout 2020 and 2021. In particular, the Asia and Pacific region saw the steepest decline in tourist arrivals among all regions in the first 5 months of 2021, with a 95% drop compared with the same period in 2019 (UNWTO 2021a). Taking into account potential renewed waves of the virus and the pandemic's implications for travel logistics (e.g., the need to harmonize travel measures across countries), international tourist flows are expected to remain below their prepandemic levels until 2024 (UNWTO 2021b).

Chapter 3

Social Protection
and Labor Policy
Response

3 Key Findings

Before the pandemic, social protection systems in Southeast Asia were weak, with large gaps in coverage linked to widespread informality.

In response to the devastating impacts of the COVID-19 crisis on jobs and incomes, governments in the region implemented sizable fiscal packages.

Social protection has constituted the lion's share of the fiscal response in Indonesia, Malaysia, the Philippines, Thailand, and Viet Nam.

Social assistance measures—in particular, large-scale cash and in-kind transfers to compensate for income losses and sustain livelihoods—were the largest component of the social protection response in these countries.

Social insurance, which has a narrow reach in the region, was only a small part of the response, emphasizing the need to tackle persistent informality.

All five countries attempted to fill gaps in social protection, extending it to vulnerable groups such as youth, informal workers, the self-employed, and migrant workers.

The speed and timeliness of interventions were aided by the use of social registries or beneficiary databases from existing programs and electronic methods for disbursing benefits.

Pandemic spending has narrowed the fiscal space for sustained interventions, but the crisis is far from over. A gradual phasing out of emergency measures must be coupled with greater investment in social protection infrastructure, to sustain inclusive growth and improve resilience.

Active labor market policies—such as the wage and training subsidies carried out across all five countries—will continue to help widen access to decent work opportunities in the future, as technology and trade continue to shape labor markets.

Before the pandemic, Southeast Asia had limited effective social protection coverage

SDG 1.3.1: Population protected in at least one area of social protection

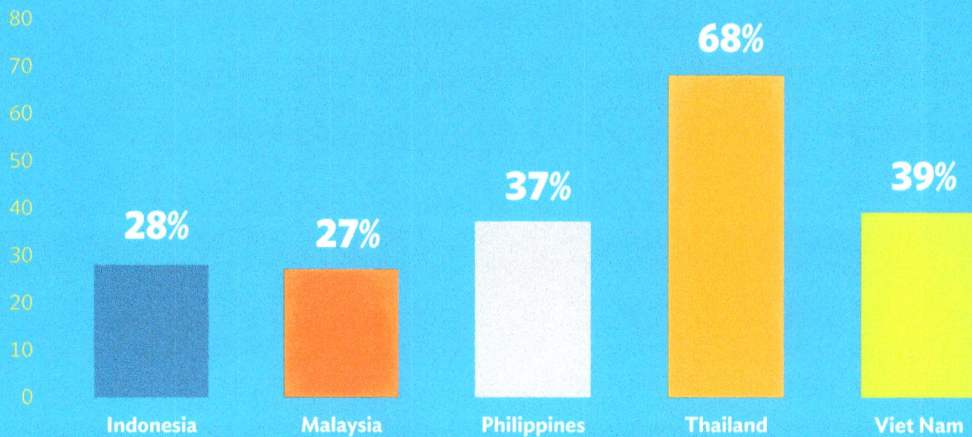

Indonesia	Malaysia	Philippines	Thailand	Viet Nam
28%	27%	37%	68%	39%

But as COVID-19 destroyed jobs and pushed millions below the poverty line, the social protection response across the region was significant.

THAILAND
Rao Mai Ting Kan Program provided subsidies to **39%** of informal workers

Rao Chana Social Assistance Program covered around **50%** of the population

VIET NAM
Nearly **40%** of the population received cash payments

PHILIPPINES
Social Amelioration Program expanded its coverage from **17% to 69%** of the population

MALAYSIA
Employment Retention Program covered **24%** of the workforce, with one-third of the population receiving social assistance

INDONESIA
80% of beneficiaries of the BLT Village Fund Cash Assistance Program were low-income families who had never received government assistance

While the COVID-19 crisis had substantial labor market and socioeconomic repercussions, policy response was commensurate with the impacts. Social protection, broadly defined as policies to protect jobs and support incomes, constituted an integral part of the response. Although social protection systems in Southeast Asia were already weak before the pandemic, governments implemented as many as 91 policy interventions since the onset of the crisis, including 81 interventions in our sample of five countries—Indonesia, Malaysia, the Philippines, Thailand, and Viet Nam.[1] Of these measures, social assistance comprised 43%, labor market and employment protection 38%, and social insurance 19%.

This chapter discusses the social protection response of these five countries and gives a tentative assessment of the policy measures, by juxtaposing them with the labor market impact and adjustment patterns discussed in the previous chapters. Without the extensive data and sophisticated techniques required to undertake a rigorous analysis of the policies' effectiveness in protecting jobs and incomes, we nevertheless attempt a comparative analysis of these policy responses, in terms of their timeliness, coverage, adequacy, and the extent to which they have filled preexisting social protection gaps and reached the most vulnerable population segments, such as informal workers and the working poor and their households. Section 3.1 describes prepandemic social protection gaps in Southeast Asia, while section 3.2 examines the social protection policy response to COVID-19 in our sample countries, covering three categories of policies: labor market and employment protection (section 3.2.1), social assistance (section 3.2.2), and social insurance (section 3.3.3).

In this chapter, the data on legal and effective social protection coverage were obtained from the World Social Protection Report Database[2] of the International Labour Organization (ILO), while data on coverage, adequacy, and incidence to the poorest population segments are from the World Bank's Atlas of Social Protection – Indicators of Resilience and Equity database.[3] To assess policy responses, we use data primarily from the International Policy Centre for Inclusive Growth's database, Social Protection Responses to COVID-19 in the Global South, supplemented by data from ADB's COVID-19 Policy Database[4] and the ILO's Social Protection Monitor.[5]

Social Protection before the Pandemic

Before the COVID-19 pandemic, Southeast Asia already had major social protection gaps. Among the five sample countries covered in this study, social insurance (contributory social protection programs) for unemployed persons existed under the form of unemployment insurance in Thailand and Viet Nam, and as severance payments in the other three countries (Table 3.1). Maternity benefits were covered by social insurance in the Philippines and in Viet Nam, through employer liability in Indonesia and Malaysia, and through both social insurance and employer

---

[1]   International Policy Centre for Inclusive Growth. Social Protection Responses to COVID-19 in the Global South Online Dashboard. https://socialprotection.org/social-protection-responses-covid-19-global-south (accessed 28 May 2021). Table A3.1–A3.3 provide a detailed description of selected policy interventions implemented in our sample of five countries including the program's timeliness, coverage, adequacy, and budget cost and funding source.

[2]   International Labour Organization (ILO). World Social Protection Database. https://www.social-protection.org/gimi/WSPDB.action?id=32 (accessed 9 November 2021).

[3]   World Bank. The Atlas of Social Protection: Indicators of Resilience and Equity. https://databank.worldbank.org/source/1229 (accessed 7 May 2021).

[4]   Asian Development Bank (ADB). ADB COVID-19 Policy Database. https://data.adb.org/dataset/adb-covid-19-policy-database (accessed 12 November 2021).

[5]   International Labour Organization (ILO). Social Protection Monitor: announced measures throughout the world. https://www.social-protection.org/gimi/ShowWiki.action?id=3426 (accessed 9 November 2021).

liability in Thailand. Social insurance for disability or invalidity was available in all five countries, as well as old-age pensions through either social insurance or provident funds. Effective social protection coverage[6] remained generally low across most social protection areas (Figure 3.1). The share of the population effectively covered by at least one area of social protection (Sustainable Development Goal indicator 1.3.1) in 2020 or the latest year available was 27% for Malaysia, 28% for Indonesia, 37% for the Philippines, 39% for Viet Nam, and 68% for Thailand (ILO 2021f).

Although social insurance programs are part of national protection systems in these countries, they have limited population coverage (Figure 3.2) due to the prevalence of informal work including employment in the informal and household sectors, as well as informal employment in the formal sector in most countries. Few programs include self-employed workers, and when this is the case, coverage is either through voluntary contributions or benefit amounts are relatively small (Table 3.1). Because they cover primarily those in formal wage employment, these programs reached only less than 4% of the poorest quintile across the region's countries.

Table 3.1: Overview of Social Protection Systems, Selected Countries

		Indonesia	Malaysia	Philippines	Thailand	Viet Nam
Child and Family	Social assistance	✓				✓
	Social insurance				✓	✓
Maternity	Social insurance			✓	✓	✓
	Employer liability	✓	✓		✓	
Self-employed covered?		No	No	Yes	Yes, voluntary basis	No
Unemployment	Social insurance				✓	✓
	Severance payment	✓	✓	✓		
Employment injury	Social insurance	✓	✓	✓		✓
	Employer liability				✓(involving insurance with a public carrier)	✓(temporary disability benefits)
Self-employed covered?		Yes, 1% of monthly declared earnings	Yes	No	No	No
Disability/ invalidity	Social insurance	✓	✓	✓	✓	✓
	Provident fund	✓	✓		✓	✓
	Social assistance					✓
Old age	Social insurance	✓		✓	✓	✓
	Provident fund	✓	✓		✓	
	Social assistance		✓	✓	✓	✓

Notes: The table is based on the compilation of various key features of social protection programs of selected Southeast Asian countries from ILO's World Social Protection Database.
Source: Authors' compilation using ILO's World Social Protection Database. https://www.social protection.org/gimi/WSPDB.action?id=32 (accessed 9 November 2021).

---

[6]   Social protection indicators published by the ILO distinguish between legal coverage and effective coverage, respectively measuring the population groups covered by a social protection area in existing national legislation, and those covered in practice (who are either contributing to a social insurance scheme or receiving benefits from it) (ILO 2017).

Figure 3.1: Effective Coverage by Social Protection Area, Selected Countries

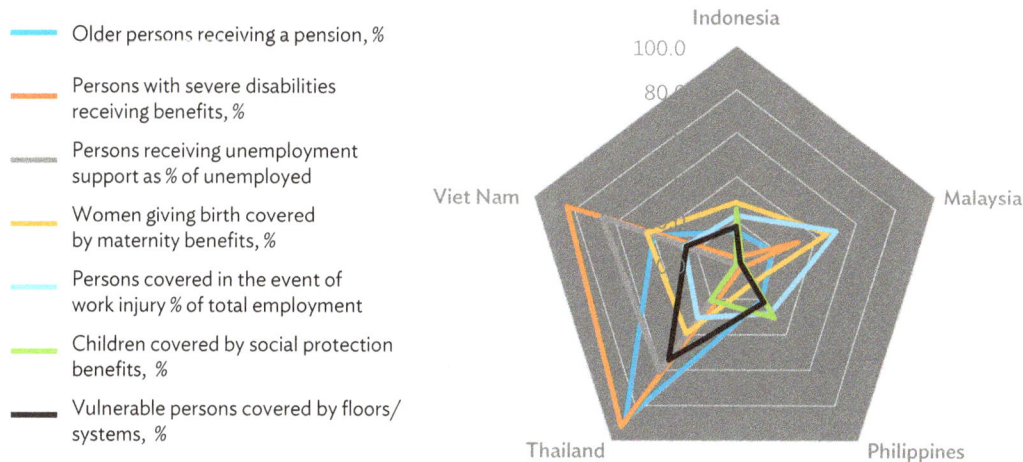

Older persons receiving a pension, %

Persons with severe disabilities receiving benefits, %

Persons receiving unemployment support as % of unemployed

Women giving birth covered by maternity benefits, %

Persons covered in the event of work injury % of total employment

Children covered by social protection benefits, %

Vulnerable persons covered by floors/ systems, %

Note: Effective protection refers to the share of the relevant population who is either actively contributing to a social insurance program, or receiving benefits.
Source: ILO (2021f).

Social assistance (non-contributory programs or social safety nets) had higher population coverage and higher incidence to the poorest quintile, but limited adequacy of benefits, as measured by the benefits' share in the total welfare of beneficiary households (Figure 3.2). When all social protection measures, including labor programs are taken into account, population coverage improves, but the adequacy of benefits and the incidence to the poorest quintile remain minimal.

Despite considerable poverty reduction across the region in the decade preceding the pandemic, a large number of workers still lived with their households just above the poverty line in the moderately poor or near-poor categories (see Chapter 1). These workers, often informal, are usually neither covered by social insurance nor targeted by social assistance—a group referred to in the literature as the "missing middle" (ILO 2017; ESCAP–ILO 2021b). The pandemic further highlighted the vulnerability of these workers. ILO estimates indicate that an additional 2 million workers and their households have fallen below the extreme poverty line, and another 1.6 million workers below the moderate poverty line in the Asia and Pacific region in 2020 (ILO forthcoming).[7]

Compounding these social protection gaps was limited access to health care in many countries. With the exception of Thailand, where 98% of the population was affiliated with a health insurance scheme, private out-of-pocket health expenditure as a share of total health expenditure was high across the region, with 35% in Malaysia and Indonesia, 45% in Viet Nam, and as much as 54% in the Philippines in 2018.[8] In Viet Nam, 0.25% of the population was pushed below the $1.90 ($ 2011 PPP) poverty line by out-of-pocket health-care expenditure in 2016.[9]

---

[7]　The extreme and moderate working poor categories refer to workers living in households with a daily per capita income or consumption of less than $1.90 and between $1.90 and $3.20, respectively, in purchasing power parity (PPP) terms. These correspond to the most recent ILO estimates, revised downward, due in part to heavy job losses among the working poor, which partly offset the net increase in their numbers (ILO, forthcoming).

[8]　World Bank. World Development Indicators. https://databank.worldbank.org/source/world-development-indicators (accessed 2 December 2021). ILO. World Social Protection Database. https://www.social protection.org/gimi/WSPDB. action?id=32 (accessed 9 November 2021).

[9]　World Bank. World Development Indicators. https://databank.worldbank.org/source/world-development-indicators (accessed 2 December 2021).

Figure 3.2: Social Protection and Labor Programs – Coverage, Adequacy, and Benefit Incidence to the Poorest, Selected Countries

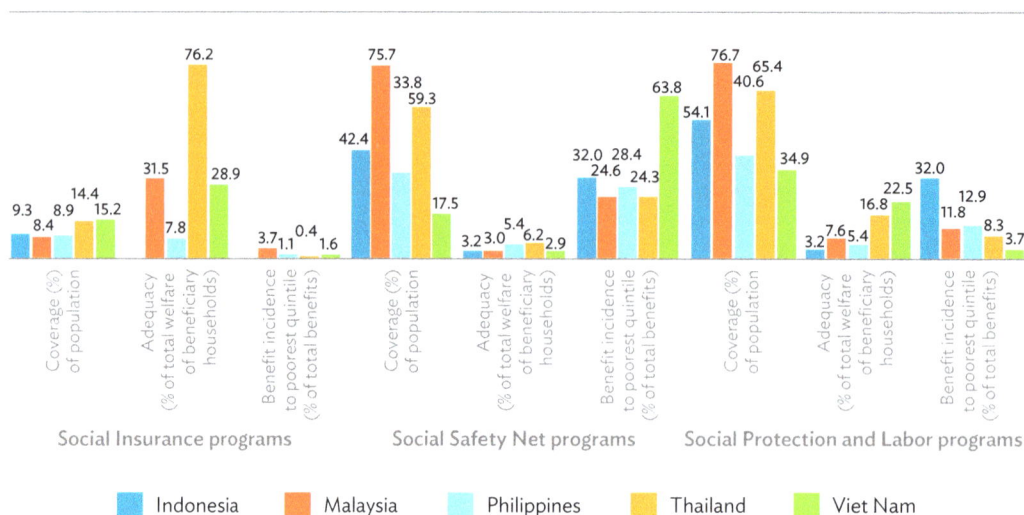

Source: World Bank. The Atlas of Social Protection: Indicators of Resilience and Equity. https://databank.worldbank.org/source/1229 (accessed 7 May 2021).

What Policies Have Mitigated the Impact?

In the first phase of the COVID-19 crisis, which reached its peak in the second quarter (Q2) of 2020, most countries in the region imposed strict and stringent lockdown and containment measures. Although these measures played a crucial role in containing the spread of the virus, they also affected workers and enterprises (see Chapters 1 and 2). To prevent further macroeconomic decline, help businesses stay afloat, and offset working hour and income losses, many governments implemented significant policy response packages including monetary and fiscal policies.

In general, the availability of fiscal space (Box 3.1) was a key determinant of the fiscal response to the COVID-19 crisis worldwide. In particular, advanced economies with less financing constraints were able to allocate more resources than emerging and developing economies. And yet, expenditure on the fiscal response packages announced since the onset of the pandemic has been significant in Southeast Asia, ranging from 2.7% of gross domestic product (GDP) in Viet Nam to 18.8% of GDP in Thailand (Figure 3.3). These fiscal packages included additional spending or forgone revenue on health and income support (above the line measures) as well as liquidity support in the form of equity injections, loans, asset purchases, and guarantees (below the line measures).

Across Southeast Asia, social protection was a key component of the response. The social protection portion of fiscal packages, using spending on health and income support measures as a proxy, has been substantial, making up around 65% in Malaysia and Viet Nam, 77% in Thailand, 88% in the Philippines, and 91% in Indonesia.[10]

---

[10] Authors' calculations based on the International Monetary Fund. Database of Fiscal Policy Responses to COVID-19. https://www.imf.org/en/Topics/imf-and-covid19/Fiscal-Policies-Database-in-Response-to-COVID-19 (accessed 18 November 2021).

Figure 3.3: Fiscal Response to COVID-19 as a Percentage of GDP, Selected Countries and Country Groups

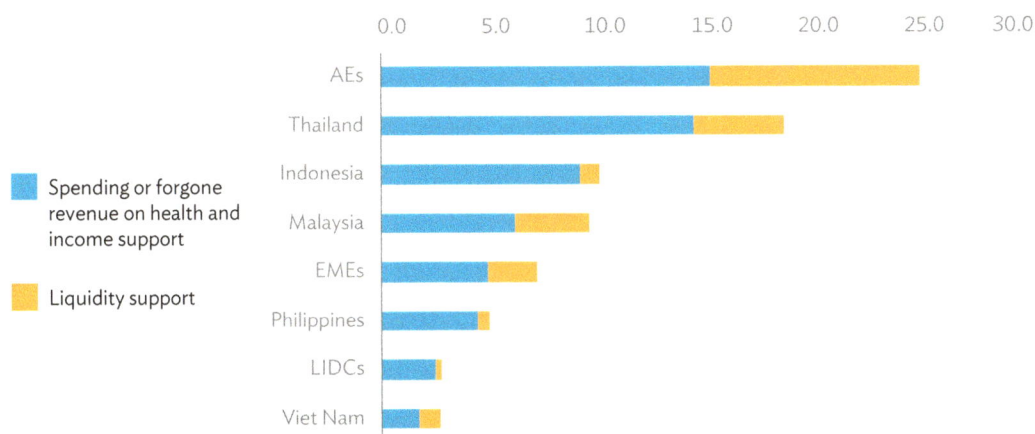

Spending or forgone revenue on health and income support

Liquidity support

AEs = advanced economies, EMEs = emerging market economies, LIDCs = low-income developing countries
Note: Estimates are as of 27 September 2021. Country group averages are weighted by GDP in US dollars adjusted by purchasing power parity.
Source: International Monetary Fund. Database of Fiscal Policy Responses to COVID-19. https://www.imf.org/en/Topics/imf-and-covid19/Fiscal-Policies-Database-in-Response-to-COVID-19 (accessed 18 November 2021).

Figure 3.4: Fiscal Space and the COVID-19 Response, 2019–2020

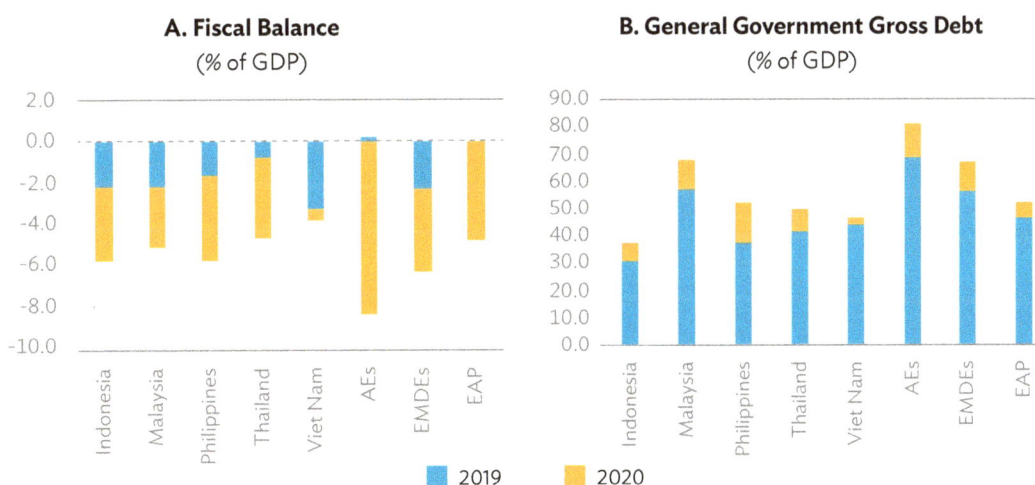

A. Fiscal Balance (% of GDP)

B. General Government Gross Debt (% of GDP)

2019   2020

AEs = advanced economies, EAP = East Asia and the Pacific , EMDEs = emerging and developing economies, GDP = gross domestic product.
Source: World Bank. A Cross-Country Database of Fiscal Space. http://www.worldbank.org/en/research/brief/fiscal-space (accessed 18 November 2021).

The substantial expenditure on COVID-19 response in 2020 has further narrowed the fiscal space in these countries, as reflected by widening budget deficits and increased public debt (Figure 3.4). Among the sample countries, additional spending weighed on fiscal space most severely in the Philippines, where government debt as a share of GDP increased by as much as 40% in 2020. Indeed, the Philippines is among the countries where cash transfers, while substantial in 2020, may have fallen short of what is need in 2021 (World Bank 2021c). Viet Nam had the lowest level of spending in 2020 and was least affected in terms of narrowing fiscal space. The increase in government debt as a share of GDP in Indonesia, Malaysia, and Thailand was close to the average of emerging and developing economies.

Box 3.1: COVID-19 Fiscal Space and Social Protection in Southeast Asia

The COVID-19 pandemic has led to significant fiscal spending across the world. In contrast with advanced economies, emerging and developing economies were more constrained in terms of fiscal space, which was in turn further limited by spending incurred during the pandemic. But what is fiscal space and why is it so important?

Fiscal space is a complex concept, as evidenced by multiple definitions used in the literature. It has been defined as the budgetary room available to create and allocate funding for a purpose without threatening liquidity and financial sustainability for instance by Heller (2005) and Ley (2009); an alternative means of expressing a government's intertemporal budget constraint by Perotti (2007); the current level of debt and a country-specific debt limit by Ostry et al. (2010); and through one of its core aspects—a government's ability to service its debts by Kose et al. (2017).

The International Labour Organization, the United Nations Children's Fund (UNICEF), and UN WOMEN broadly define fiscal space as the resources available to the government from all revenue sources, which can be used to implement policies and provide eight financing options to expand countries' fiscal space for social protection (Ortiz et al. 2019; Duran-Valverde et al. 2020). Box Table 3.1 provides some indicators to assess these financing options in the context of Indonesia, Malaysia, the Philippines, Thailand, and Viet Nam. Before the pandemic, countries in the region adopted some of these strategies. For instance, Indonesia and Thailand both attempted to expand social security contributions and implement accommodative macroeconomic policies and, in Thailand, efforts were made to reduce debt or debt servicing (Ortiz et al. 2019). Different financing options or strategies have their advantages, and their feasibility depends on the country context and timing.

Expanding social security coverage and contributory revenues is crucial but challenging in the countries of the region, given widespread informality. It goes hand in hand with efforts to formalize the economy. Examples of successful policies in this regard include Uruguay's Monotax and other policies in Argentina and Brazil (Duran-Valverde et al. 2020; Megersa 2019).

While tax revenues as a share of GDP are higher in these economies than in other emerging and developing economies (EMDEs) on average, this share remains well below the average of advanced economies. Tax revenues can be further decomposed into various sources, to identify areas where potential additional revenue from taxation is highest. Most middle-income countries in the region still rely primarily on indirect taxes and could have important gains from more progressive taxation through increased use of direct taxes, including corporate and personal income taxes and wealth taxes (World Bank 2021c). Taxation has benefits beyond its role as a financing option: its potential positive impacts on government legitimacy and accountability which could set in motion a virtuous circle whereby tax collection is associated with better service delivery and therefore leads to an increase in citizens' willingness to pay taxes (Megersa 2019). Regional and international cooperation for taxation can help in mobilizing domestic revenue, in a context of capital mobility (World Bank 2021c).

While more recent data are not available, 2004–2013 estimates suggest that there is significant fiscal space to be gained through curbing illicit financial flows from these countries. Malaysia, Thailand, and Indonesia ranked 5th, 8th, and 9th, respectively, among all developing and emerging economies in terms of the largest average illicit financial flows (in millions of US dollars) during 2004–2013 (Kar and Spanjers 2015).

Social protection expenditure as a share of GDP is lower in the sample countries than the upper-middle-income average. This suggests that there is room for budget reallocation toward social protection spending. During the COVID-19 pandemic, many countries in Southeast Asia reallocated resources toward social protection, including Indonesia, Malaysia, and the Philippines.

Although the fiscal deficit increased for all the sample countries in 2020, the increases were within the range of other countries. Inflation patterns differed across the sample countries, but generally, inflation remained within central bank targets. One exception is the Philippines, where inflation lies slightly above the upper bound of the official target (World Bank 2021c). In general, conditions permit the continuation of accommodative macro policies in these countries.

Indonesia, Malaysia, and Thailand which are upper-middle-income countries, are not net recipients of official development assistance (ODA). In the Philippines and Viet Nam, net ODA receipts represented 0.22% and 0.44% of GNI, respectively, in 2019. Concessional external debt stocks as a share of gross domestic debt are far lower than the regional and EMDEs average, except for Viet Nam. Although there may be room to expand fiscal space for social protection through external sources, domestic resource mobilization should be prioritized, as it is more stable and sustainable.

Sources: Ortiz et al. (2019); Duran-Valverde et al. (2020); Kose et al. (2017); (World Bank 2021c).

continued on next page

Box 3.1 continued

Box Table 3.1: Financing Options for Social Protection and Selected Indicators
for Indonesia, Malaysia, the Philippines, Thailand, and Viet Nam

Financing Options	Indicators	Indonesia	Malaysia	Philippines	Thailand	Viet Nam	Comparative Measures
Expanding social security coverage and contributory revenues	Social contributions (% of revenue),[a] 2019	...	...	...	5.3	...	High-income countries average: 30.4 Upper-middle-income countries average: 6.8
Increasing tax revenues	Tax revenues (% of GDP),[b] 2020	11.8	15.2	14.3	16.2	15.1	EAP average: 15.0 AEs average: 22.0% EMDEs average: 10.5%
Eliminating illicit financial flows	Illicit financial flows (% of GDP),[c] 2004–2013 average	3.1	18.6	4.9	6.5	9.0	
Reallocating public expenditures	Social protection expenditure (% of GDP)[d]	1.3	4.2	2.6	3.0	4.3	Southeast Asia: 2.5 Upper-middle-income countries: 8.0
Tapping into fiscal and foreign exchange reserves	Total reserves (% of total external debt)	32.6	...	111.7	126.4	75.8	EAP average: 121.8 EMDEs average: 88.7
Managing debt (borrowing or restructuring)	Total debt service (% of GNI), 2020	6.5	...	2.4	3.5	6.4	
Adopting a more accommodative macroeconomic framework	Fiscal balance (% of GDP),[b] 2020	-5.9	-5.2	-5.7	-4.7	-3.9	EAP average: -4.8 AEs average: -8.1 EMDEs average: -6.4
	Inflation, consumer prices (annual %),[a] 2020	1.9	-1.1	2.6	-0.8	3.2	High-income countries: 0.5 Upper-middle-income countries: 2.2
Increasing aid and transfers	Net ODA received (% of GNI),[a] 2019	-0.06	0.00	0.22	-0.06	0.44	EAP: 0.03
	Concessional external debt stocks (% of general government gross debt)[b]	2.8	...	4.2	1.1	18.7	EAP average: 24.0 EMDEs average: 18.4

... = data not available, AEs = advanced economies, EAP = East Asia and the Pacific, EMDEs = emerging and developing economies, GDP = gross domestic product, GNI = gross national income, ODA = official development assistance.
Note: Financing options listed in the table are based on Ortiz et al. (2019) and Duran-Valverde et al. (2020).
[a] World Bank. World Development Indicators. https://databank.worldbank.org/source/world-development-indicators (accessed 2 December 2021).
[b] World Bank. A Cross-Country Database of Fiscal Space. http://www.worldbank.org/en/research/brief/fiscal-space (accessed 18 November 2021).
[c] Kar and Spanjers (2015).
[d] ILO. World Social Protection Database. https://www.social protection.org/gimi/WSPDB.action?id=32 (accessed 9 November 2021).
Source: Authors' compilation.

As illustrated in Figure 3.5, the largest number of measures and allocated budget amounts were announced early on in the crisis, between March and June 2020, with countries implementing additional measures, extending the duration of programs, and increasing their spending commitments and budgets over time, as well as reallocating funds towards social protection throughout 2020 and 2021. Budget reallocation and the reprioritization of spending are important means of expanding fiscal space to respond to the crisis. Box 3.1 discusses the importance of expanding fiscal space for social protection, as well as strategies to achieve this.

The policy mix used in each country reflects the local context and preexisting strengths and weaknesses of social protection systems. In Indonesia, social assistance measures accounted for much of the policy response. In Malaysia, the Philippines, and Thailand, these policies were accompanied by an equivalent number of labor market policies. In Viet Nam, labor market and employment policies represented half of the COVID-19 social protection response. All countries in our sample implemented cash-based transfers and provided subsidies or financial assistance for housing or utilities (Table 3.2). All countries introduced some form of wage subsidy as well. Other widely used measures were paid leave or unemployment insurance and other labor market policies. Even within the same category, however, interventions differed greatly along several dimensions, such as scope (new intervention, horizontal or vertical expansion of existing measures, implementation change),[11] population or labor force coverage (targeted or actual), duration, etc.

We first consider labor market and employment protection policies that are aimed at preserving jobs during the pandemic, before we look at social assistance for supporting incomes and livelihoods. We also discuss social insurance, although it is a less significant part of the COVID-19 response in these countries, as strengthening and expanding social insurance alongside policies that promote formalization, will be crucial for enhancing the inclusiveness, resilience, and sustainability of social protection systems in these countries in the long run.

---

[11]   Horizontal expansion refers to coverage or number of beneficiaries. Vertical expansion refers to an increase in the benefit amount. An implementation change can involve relaxing eligibility criteria, advancing payments, deferring contributions, etc.

Figure 3.5: COVID-19 Response Measures and Financial Resource Allocation in Selected Countries, April 2020 – October 2021

($ millions)

Thailand
- Aid program for returning Thai workers from the Republic of Korea
- Social Security Agency to cover treatment costs for all COVID-19 patients
- Reduced contributions to the SSF by employers and employees
- Cash benefit for low-income HHs
- Wage subsidies to SMEs
- Cash transfer of B5,000 ($153) for 3 months for workers not covered by the SSF
- Increased unemployment compensation
- Welfare card holders will get financial assistance

Indonesia
- Financial benefits to low-income HHs for 6 months
- Enhancing subsidized housing program, mortgage subsidies
- Reallocation of funds to social assistance measures
- Rp3.5 trillion to subsidize electricity bills
- Expanded budget and benefits of Indonesia's flagship CCT program
- Budget allocation to subsidize social contributions to health insurance
- Rp600,000 cash transfer to HHs in need
- Cash benefit for 197,000 taxi drivers and bus operators
- Double allocated budget for Kartu Prakerja program
- Increasing coverage and benefits of the food voucher program Sembako for 9 months
- Rp16.9 trillion to cash for work programs

Malaysia
- Extension of social security coverage to domestic helpers
- ihsan Johor 3.0 financial aid package to manage the pandemic and strengthen social security
- Social Security Organisation disbursed RM11.11 million to eligible contributors who died of COVID-19.

Malaysia
- Prioritization of welfare in 2021's budget
- Withdrawals allowed from EPF to assist members affected by the pandemic

Viet Nam
- No fees for persons under mandatory quarantine in health centers
- Patients with chronic diseases to receive medicine in advance
- Allowance for people fighting COVID-19
- Special monthly allowance to poor HHs, and workers affected by COVID-19
- Payment of social security benefits at home
- Electricity prices reduced for 3 months
- Deferral of social contributions for affected firms and workers

Indonesia
- Salary subsidy to workers
- Expands wage subsidy to include 3 million additional workers
- Extension of free electricity until December

Philippines
- Launch of online cash relief system

Thailand
- Reduced mandatory SSF contributions for 3 months
- Compensation for employees who cannot work due to the Second Wave of COVID-19 (3 months)

Malaysia
- Temporary reduction in the employee contribution rate to the EPF for members younger than age 60
- EPF started allowing members younger than age 55 to withdraw a portion of their account

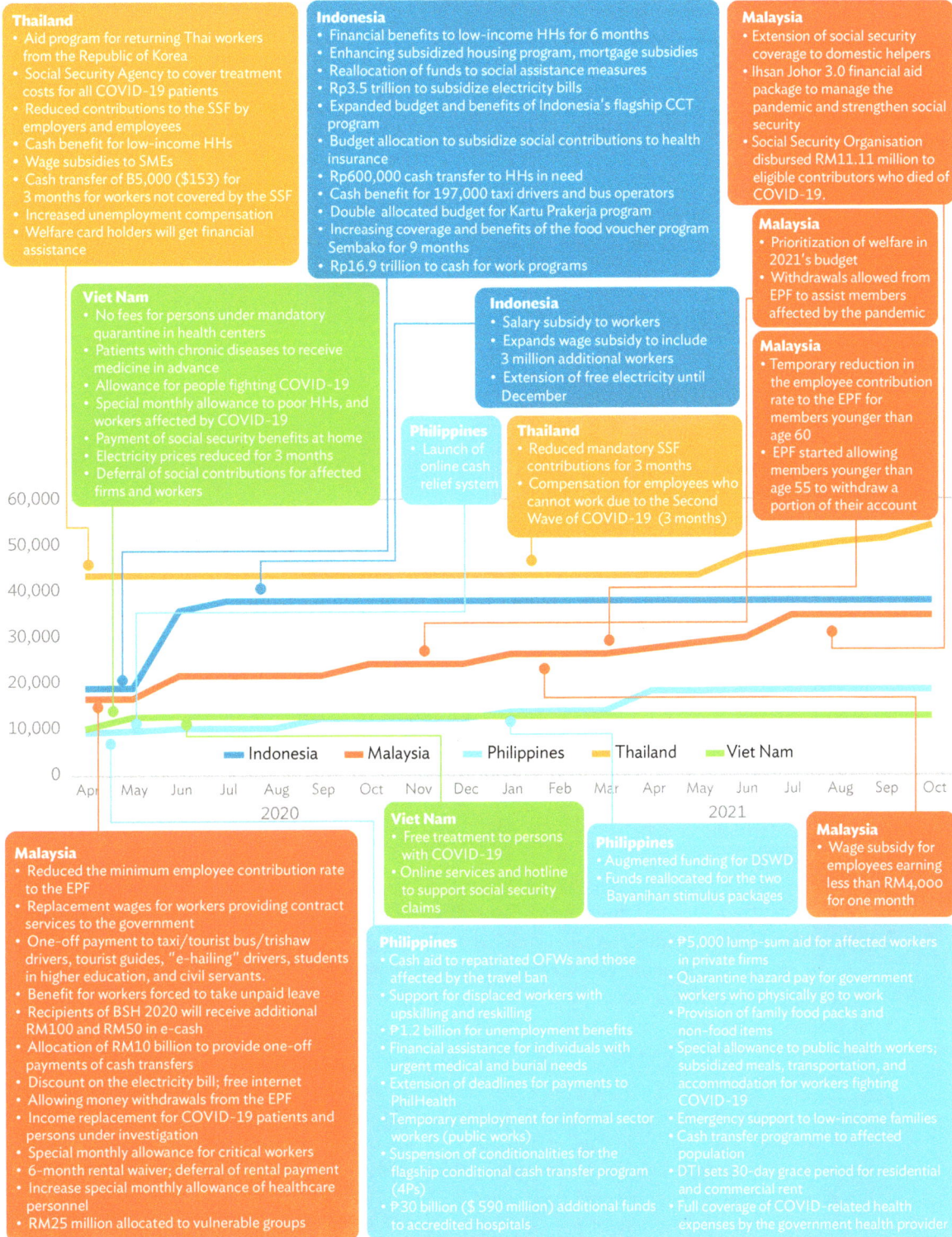

| | Indonesia | Malaysia | Philippines | Thailand | Viet Nam |

Apr May Jun Jul Aug Sep Oct Nov Dec Jan Feb Mar Apr May Jun Jul Aug Sep Oct
2020 — 2021

Viet Nam
- Free treatment to persons with COVID-19
- Online services and hotline to support social security claims

Philippines
- Augmented funding for DSWD
- Funds reallocated for the two Bayanihan stimulus packages

Malaysia
- Wage subsidy for employees earning less than RM4,000 for one month

Malaysia
- Reduced the minimum employee contribution rate to the EPF
- Replacement wages for workers providing contract services to the government
- One-off payment to taxi/tourist bus/trishaw drivers, tourist guides, "e-hailing" drivers, students in higher education, and civil servants.
- Benefit for workers forced to take unpaid leave
- Recipients of BSH 2020 will receive additional RM100 and RM50 in e-cash
- Allocation of RM10 billion to provide one-off payments of cash transfers
- Discount on the electricity bill; free internet
- Allowing money withdrawals from the EPF
- Income replacement for COVID-19 patients and persons under investigation
- Special monthly allowance for critical workers
- 6-month rental waiver; deferral of rental payment
- Increase special monthly allowance of healthcare personnel
- RM25 million allocated to vulnerable groups

Philippines
- Cash aid to repatriated OFWs and those affected by the travel ban
- Support for displaced workers with upskilling and reskilling
- P1.2 billion for unemployment benefits
- Financial assistance for individuals with urgent medical and burial needs
- Extension of deadlines for payments to PhilHealth
- Temporary employment for informal sector workers (public works)
- Suspension of conditionalities for the flagship conditional cash transfer program (4Ps)
- P30 billion ($ 590 million) additional funds to accredited hospitals

- P5,000 lump-sum aid for affected workers in private firms
- Quarantine hazard pay for government workers who physically go to work
- Provision of family food packs and non-food items
- Special allowance to public health workers; subsidized meals, transportation, and accommodation for workers fighting COVID-19
- Emergency support to low-income families
- Cash transfer programme to affected population
- DTI sets 30-day grace period for residential and commercial rent
- Full coverage of COVID-related health expenses by the government health provider

4Ps = Pantawid Pamilyang Pilipino Program, DSWD = Department of Social Welfare and Development, EPF = Employees Provident Fund, HHs = households, SMEs = small and medium enterprises, SSF = Social Security Fund.

Sources: ILO. World Social Protection Database. https://www.social protection.org/gimi/WSPDB.action?id=32 (accessed 9 November 2021); Asian Development Bank (ADB). ADB COVID-19 Policy Database. https://data.adb.org/dataset/adb-covid-19-policy-database (accessed 12 November 2021).

Table 3.2: Social Protection and Labor Market Policy Response to COVID-19, Measures Implemented in Selected Countries since the Onset of the Crisis

	Indonesia	Malaysia	Philippines	Thailand	Viet Nam
Social assistance (non-contributory)					
Cash- based transfers	✓	✓	✓	✓	✓
Public works	✓		✓		
In-kind (in- kind/school feeding)	✓	✓	✓		
Housing/ basic services, utility and financial support	✓	✓	✓	✓	✓
Social insurance (contributory)					
Paid leave/unemployment	✓	✓	✓	✓	
Health insurance support	✓		✓	✓	✓
Pensions		✓			✓
Social security contributions (waiver/subsidy)		✓		✓	✓
Labor markets					
Wage subsidies/ allowance for temporary work suspension	✓	✓	✓	✓	✓
LM activation and training	✓	✓	✓	✓	
Labor regulation	✓				

Notes: Labor regulation measures in Indonesia included the provision of guidance on worker protection and business sustenance through circulars, data collection and monitoring of layoffs, strengthening the role of labor attaches to ensure adequate implementation of WHO protocol, and extending work permits of foreign workers.
Sources: International Labour Organization (ILO). World Social Protection Database. https://www.social-protection.org/gimi/WSPDB. action?id=32 (accessed 9 November 2021); Gentilini et al. (2021).

Labor market and employment protection policies

In examining labor market policies, we focus on wage subsidies and other measures and incentives meant to restrain job losses and maintain employment relationships. In our sample of countries, Malaysia and the Philippines were the first to announce wage subsidy programs for workers by the end of March 2020, followed by Thailand and Viet Nam in early April 2020, and Indonesia in August 2020.

In Malaysia, through the Employment Retention Program, the government subsidized wages of employees insured under the Social Security Organization (SOCSO) Employment Insurance Scheme (EIS) to assist employers in retaining their workers during the crisis. This policy covered 25% of the labor force, with a subsidy equivalent to 38.6% of the average wage (Figure 3.6). The policy was rolled out in two phases, with a budget of RM5.9 billion for the first phase, and RM2.4 billion for the second. The program targeted lower pay workers who earn RM4,000 or less and contribute to the SOCSO EIS; and whose employers are affected by the pandemic, registered with the Companies Commission Malaysia or a relevant local authority and do not retrench workers, and impose unpaid leave or force wage cuts.[12] In the second phase of the program, participating employers were still not allowed to retrench workers earning less than RM4,000, but were allowed to reduce working hours and wages through negotiations with workers. The program was accompanied by a range of additional interventions and targeted measures. In March 2020, targeted measures included

---

[12] In the first phase, affected employers were those experiencing more than 50% decrease in their income since 1 January 2020. In the second phase, employers still affected by the crisis are those who since the Recovery Movement Control Order were still facing lower revenues of at least 30% compared with 2019.

special allowances for frontline workers; wage subsidies for workers under service contracts with the government during the movement control order; and one-off cash incentives to taxi drivers, tour guides and trishaw drivers, and e-hailing drivers who were registered and employed. As of June 2020, additional measures included a range of tax incentives to employers offering flexible work arrangements for employees registered under the Employment Injury Scheme, and subsidies to working parents for child-care expenses. Another important policy measure, announced in June but implemented at the end of August 2020 involved government support to employers for hiring and training workers during the COVID-19 crisis. The latter policy involved wage subsidies amounting to 32.4% of average wages and covered approximately 1.9% of the workforce. Although detailed labor force survey (LFS) data are unavailable to disaggregate working hour losses in Malaysia into intensive and extensive margins, the wide range of labor market measures and the relatively high coverage of the labor force (by the Employment Retention Program in particular) suggest that the measures have contributed to curtailing job losses in Malaysia throughout 2020.

In the Philippines, the COVID-19 Adjustment Measures Program (CAMP) provided cash aid to affected workers of establishments that either implemented flexible working arrangements or suspended business operations due to the pandemic. The program covered over 650,000 workers, or approximately 1.5% of the labor force, with a benefit equivalent to 34% of the average wage (Figure 3.6). CAMP was followed by the Small Business Wage Subsidy Program announced in April and implemented in May 2020, which aimed to cover 3.4 million workers, or approximately 7.5% of the labor force, employed in small businesses affected by the enhanced community quarantine. These two important subsidy programs were accompanied by more targeted ones, to support frontline public health workers and workers providing care to COVID-19 patients. These labor market and employment protection policies implemented early on in the crisis helped mitigate job losses, which were nevertheless extensive in the Philippines. Specifically, these measures may have contributed to the relatively high use of intensive margins of adjustment across most sectors in the country as described above, but the limited coverage of the labor force suggests that other factors beyond these policy interventions also played a key role.

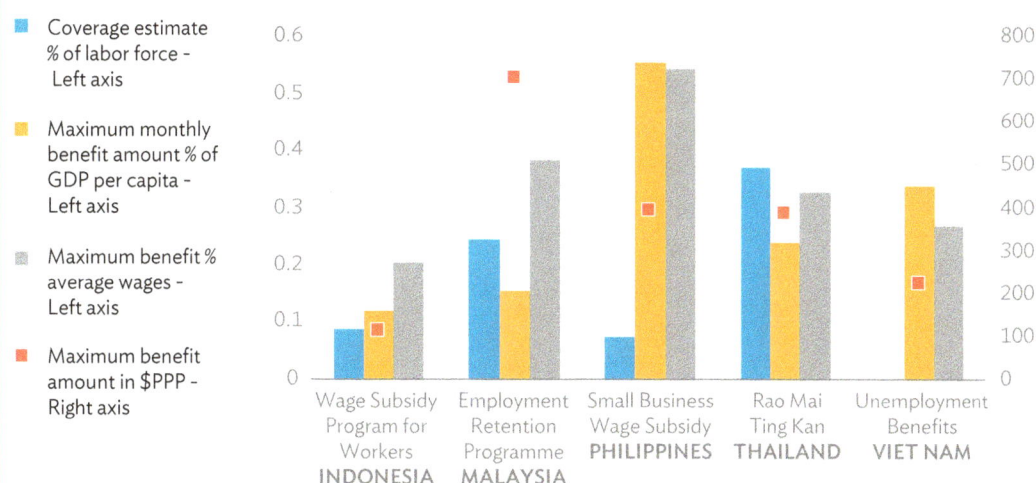

Figure 3.6: COVID-19 Labor Market Response Policies – Coverage and Adequacy of Wage Subsidies

Source: International Policy Centre for Inclusive Growth. Social Protection Responses to COVID-19 in the Global South Database. https://socialprotection.org/social-protection-responses-covid-19-global-south (accessed 28 May 2021).

Among our sample countries, Thailand suffered the least job losses in 2020. Its social security system is by far the most developed in the region, with 68% of its population effectively covered by at least one area of social protection (ILO 2021f). Consequently, Thailand's labor market policies targeted two broad groups identified as highly vulnerable to the COVID-19 pandemic: informal workers and young workers. Under the Rao Mai Ting Kan Program (No One Left Behind), informal workers (those not insured under the Social Security Fund), whether temporary contractors or self-employed workers, were eligible to receive a cash transfer for 3 months during the state of emergency. This policy covered between an estimated 14.5 million and 15.3 million workers (or 37%–39% of the workforce), with a wage subsidy equivalent to 32.9% of the average salary (Figure 3.6 and Box 3.2). Informal workers represent a large share of employment in Thailand's highly affected services sectors (wholesale and retail trade, accommodation and food services, and other services), which together accounted for 29% of job losses in Q2 2020 (Chapter 1, Table 1.1). As job losses disproportionately affected the youth in Thailand (as it did in other countries of the region), another labor market policy implemented in September 2020 aimed to protect the jobs of new graduates from universities and vocational training colleges (i.e., those under the age of 25 and who graduated before 2019), through a government subsidy equivalent to 50% of their wages. Because of its narrow target group, this policy only covered 260,000 workers or 0.7% of the workforce.

Box 3.2: Protecting Vulnerable Informal Workers – Thailand's Comprehensive and Impressive COVID-19 Social Assistance Response

More than half of Thailand's workers, or over 20 million people, are engaged in informal work.[a] This means that they are not covered by a social security scheme, regardless of whether employed in the formal, informal, or household sector. Some of the sectors that experienced the most significant disruption because of the COVID-19 crisis had the highest share of informal workers. Almost all employment in the agriculture sector is informal (90%), but informality is also very high in "other services" (71%), accommodation and food services (65%), arts and entertainment (60%), and wholesale and retail trade (55%). The containment measures also affected the livelihoods and income of informal workers most severely given their lack of income security and exclusion from most social protection measures. There are voluntary social insurance schemes for informal workers in Thailand, but these have very limited coverage. In 2019, only 15% or around 3 million informal workers made voluntary contributions to the Social Security Fund—none were eligible for unemployment insurance under the terms of their coverage (World Bank 2021a).

The lack of social security coverage for informal workers was the most significant gap exposed by the COVID-19 crisis in Thailand's social protection system. In response, the Government of Thailand mobilized new emergency programs targeted at informal workers and farmers. Under the Rao Mai Ting Kan (No One Left Behind) Program, informal workers received cash transfers of B5,000 per month for 3 months (Box Figure 3.2). This program covered an estimated 15.3 million informal workers and cost around B229.5 billion or 1.46% of GDP (Box Figure 3.2 and World Bank 2021a).

A separate cash transfer of B5,000 for 3 months was also given to farmers, fishermen, and herders already registered for preexisting forms of government assistance provided through the Bank of Agriculture and Agricultural Cooperatives (World Bank 2021a); about 7.5 million farmers received this cash transfer. Furthermore, given the increase in COVID-19 cases in late 2020 and early 2021, additional cash transfers of B3,500 per month for 2 months (February and March 2021) were paid to around 30 million informal workers, farmers, and State Welfare Card holders (Theparat, Chantanusornsiri, and Bangprapa 2021).

continued on next page

Box 3.2 continued

Box Figure 3.2: Coverage of and Expenditure on COVID-19 Social Assistance Programs in 2020

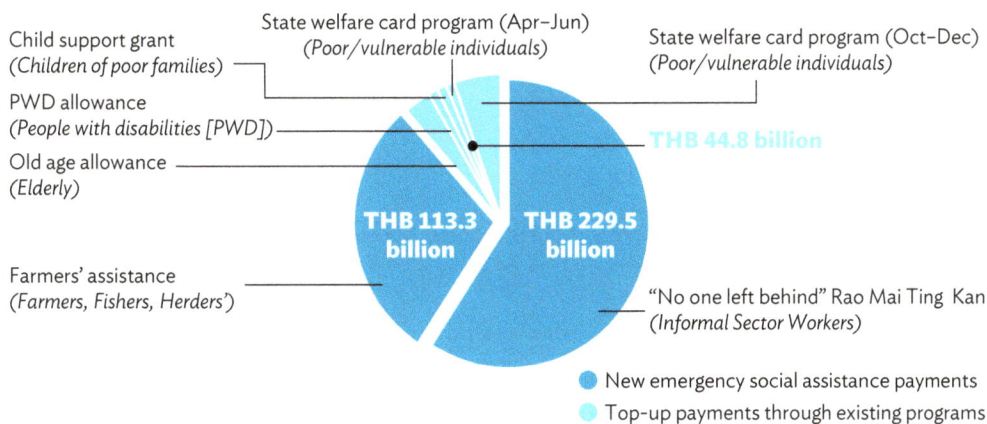

Child support grant
(Children of poor families)

State welfare card program (Apr–Jun)
(Poor/vulnerable individuals)

State welfare card program (Oct–Dec)
(Poor/vulnerable individuals)

PWD allowance
(People with disabilities [PWD])

Old age allowance
(Elderly)

THB 44.8 billion

THB 113.3 billion

THB 229.5 billion

Farmers' assistance
(Farmers, Fishers, Herders')

"No one left behind" Rao Mai Ting Kan
(Informal Sector Workers)

● New emergency social assistance payments
● Top-up payments through existing programs

Source: World Bank (2021a).

Thailand's new emergency programs for informal workers and farmers and the vertical expansion of existing social assistance schemes are comprehensive and impressive. These programs reached more than 30 million individuals—approximately 81.5% of households. According to simulations in World Bank (2021b), social protection measures have prevented a 1.2 percentage-point increase in poverty that would have occurred in 2020 sans government response. Systems already in place, such as the national ID, which helped identify new social assistance recipients and the long-established PromptPay electronic payment platform, allowed the government's swift and effective response (World Bank 2021a). Outside of the government's significant COVID-19 response effort, however, the pandemic sharpened the focus on over half of the workforce that had no social security from work. Addressing the country's persistently high levels of workforce informality remains a major challenge, one that must remain high on the government agenda, beyond the pandemic.

[a] Data on informal workers are from the Informal Employment Survey of the National Statistical Office, Ministry of Digital Economy and Society, unless otherwise specified.
[b] Theparat, Chantanusornsiri, and Bangprapa (2021).
Sources: National Statistical Office, Ministry of Digital Economy and Society; World Bank (2021a and 2021b).

In Viet Nam, the first policy to provide wage support paid an allowance to workers involved in the prevention and control of COVID-19. A broader wage subsidy program implemented from April 2020 paid unemployment benefits for a 3-month period to workers whose contract was suspended or who took unpaid leave, in cases where the employer could no longer pay wages due to the COVID-19 pandemic. The subsidy amounted to 27% of average wages (Figure 3.6). Although data on the share of the workforce covered by this policy are unavailable, coverage is likely to be somewhat limited as agricultural workers made up a large share of job losses in Q2 2020, many of whom are contributing family workers and therefore ineligible for the subsidy. Nevertheless, the wage subsidy program is likely to have benefited wage and salaried workers in the heavily affected manufacturing, wholesale and retail trade, and food and accommodation sectors.

In Indonesia, the first labor market policy response put in place in April 2020 was the Pre-Employment Card Program, through which jobseekers, laid-off workers, or workers with suspended employment contracts, among others, received cash for job training and other job incentives (see Box 3.3). The program is estimated to have covered approximately 5.5 million workers or 4.1% of the labor force by the end of 2020, with a benefit amount equivalent to 20.6% of the average wage (Box 3.3). Based on the LFS for August 2020, 28% of the population knew about the program, out of whom 7% had registered for it. Among those who did register, 13% or approximately 300,000 persons passed the selection process. Of those selected, 64% had completed training associated with the program. A large majority (89%) of those who completed training confirmed that the program improved their skills, and 84% received incentives (pocket money) from the program. LFS data therefore showed that 5 months into its implementation, the pre-employment card program had fewer beneficiaries than targeted. Despite the slow start, the program had by December 2020 almost reached its target, with approximately 5.5 million beneficiaries (see Box 3.3).

Box 3.3: Initiatives to Support Skills Development—Upskilling and Reskilling in the Time of COVID-19

Even before the COVID-19 pandemic, the rise of automation and new technologies was creating an urgent need for upskilling and reskilling in the workforce. As countries grapple with unprecedented levels of unemployment and job loss due to COVID-19, skills development and training have become even more critical. Skills development plays a key role in preparing workers for jobs of the future. This future may be approaching faster than it would have in the absence of the pandemic. In particular, considering COVID-19 as a "persistent reallocation shock" (Barrero et al. 2021) emphasizes the need for policies to facilitate transitions across sectors and occupations and highlights the importance of flexible workers being able to make such transitions. Skills development is also crucial for economic diversification, which remains key to limiting a country's vulnerability to economic shocks.

The COVID-19 pandemic has affected learning at all levels, including technical and vocational education and training (TVET) and work-based learning, due to school disruptions and closures. But it has also provided a unique opportunity for an intensified shift toward solutions that use distance learning and digital tools. Kartu Prakerja in Indonesia and free online TVET programs in the Philippines are notable examples of innovative solutions to increase the availability and accessibility of distance learning and training amid the pandemic.

The Kartu Prakerja Program, launched in April 2020, combines skills development with temporary social assistance for displaced workers and job seekers. The program provides beneficiaries with a training scholarship of Rp1,000,000 ($70.95), which they can use to purchase online courses available in the KP ecosystem (Coordinating Ministry for Economic Affairs 2021). Beneficiaries also receive a post-training incentive of Rp600,000 ($42.57) per month for 4 consecutive months. The KP Program is innovative as it uses cloud technology and end-to-end digital solutions to extend fast and reliable registration to many participants (Coordinating Ministry for Economic Affairs 2021). It also embraces a consumer-centered mindset by allowing beneficiaries to choose from various digital platforms, training providers, and types of training.

The August 2020 round of Indonesia's labor force survey included questions pertaining to the KP Program, and therefore provides some indication of the program's implementation challenges and successes. Results showed that although the program had reached less beneficiaries than targeted, around 89% of actual beneficiaries of the program reported improved skills. The program coverage subsequently expanded, reaching 5.5 million people across all provinces as of December 2020. Results of an evaluation survey showed that the program supported workers and job seekers who needed it the most. About 84% of beneficiaries had never had any training before, 82% were unemployed, and around 78% of the employed beneficiaries worked in the informal sector (Box Figure 3.3a). The program has also reached marginalized groups, including women (45%), the elderly (2%), people with disabilities (5%), those with low education (9%), people from disadvantaged regions (2%), and former migrant workers (2%).

continued on next page

Box 3.3 continued

Box Figure 3.3a: Kartu Prakerja Beneficiary Profile and Reach

84% of Kartu Prakerja Beneficiaries have never attended any training

82% of Kartu Prakerja Beneficiaries are unemployed

82% of Kartu Prakerja Beneficiaries are unemployed

IDR 1,200,000 monthly income for workers

IDR 1,000,000 monthly revenue for entrepreneurs

70% between 18–35 years old

Kartu Prakerja Program is accessible to all levels of society

2% from disadvantaged regions

45% women

2% over 60 years old

5% people with disabilities

2% former Indonesian migrant workers

9% low education, primary school, and below

Source: Coordinating Ministry for Economic Affairs of the Republic of Indonesia (2021).

The Philippines also used a digital platform, TESDA's Online Programs (TOP), to ensure continuous and greater access to training during the pandemic. TOP is an open educational resource launched in 2012 to make TVET more accessible through information and communication technology. Free online training programs form part of the government's initiative to support the retooling and upskilling of workers whose livelihoods have been affected by the pandemic.

Box Figure 3.3b: Number of New Registered Users in TESDA's Online Programs, 2012–2021

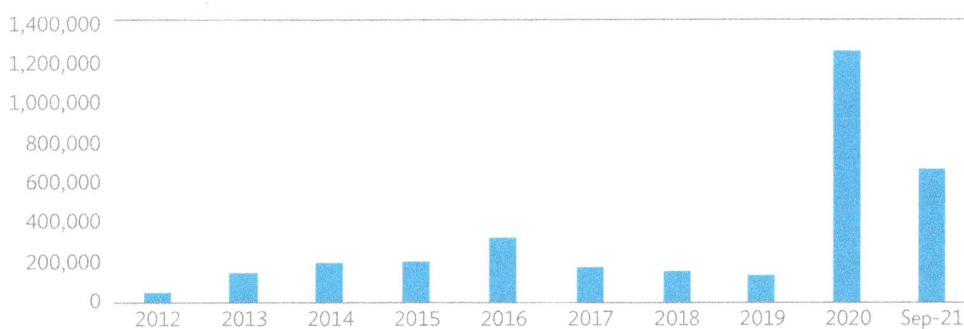

Source: TESDA (2021b).

Enrollment in TOP surged during the pandemic, with around 1.3 million registered users (Box Figure 3.3b). The number of users continued to increase in 2021, reaching 670,426 in September. The number of users from 2020 to 2021 accounted for more than half (about 58%) of the total TOP users (3.3 million) since its launch in 2012. TOP currently has 108 available online courses. Most-enrolled courses include human health/health care (37%), tourism (20%), 21st century skills (15%), electrical and electronics (10%), and entrepreneurship (5%). TESDA also proactively engaged with the private sector to boost participation in its flexible training programs. All Globe and TM mobile phone subscribers get free data access to TOP until 2022—a positive development that can reduce access barriers to online learning (TESDA 2021a). Additionally, a TESDA online program app was also created for Android and IOS gadgets to allow learners to download a course for offline use.

Sources: Coordinating Ministry for Economic Affairs of the Republic of Indonesia (2021); TESDA (2021a).

Like the other countries, Indonesia also implemented a wage subsidy, but did so with a delay relative to the others. Implemented by the end of August 2020, the measure provided wage subsidies for 4 months to active social security members with earnings of less than Rp5 million per month and covered 11.9 million workers or 8.7% of the workforce. The subsidy amount (Rp600,000 or 20.6% of the average wage) is equivalent to the benefit from the pre-employment card program. Other labor market policies in response to the pandemic were targeted, such as cash transfers to taxi, bus, and truck drivers given at the onset of the crisis in April, and wage subsidies for education personnel in November 2020, following major job losses in the education sector. Indonesia's education sector had incurred a significant share of job losses between February and August 2020 (27% of job losses, while manufacturing accounted for another 27%) (Chapter 1).

All countries in our sample have attempted, through targeted labor market measures, to fill some gaps in social protection, extending support or protection to vulnerable groups. Thailand's key policy targeted informal workers as described above. In the Philippines, the CAMP Abot Kamay ang Pagtulong sa OFWs (AKAP) targeted registered overseas Filipino workers (OFWs) affected by the pandemic, who either remained abroad or were repatriated. In 2019, there were an estimated 2.2 million OFWs, including 1.2 million women (79%) out of whom 63% were employed in elementary occupations.[13] In Indonesia, returning migrant workers were eligible for the pre-employment card program. In Malaysia, the government reduced the foreign worker levy for all companies that formally employed foreigners, to protect jobs.

In terms of timeliness and speed of interventions, policy implementation—measured by the first benefit payment in most cases, or by the date of first application/registration—was carried out early on in March–April 2020 in Malaysia, the Philippines, Thailand, and Viet Nam, and generally began within a week of the measures' announcement, and within 2 months of the first COVID-19 case in each country (mid-January 2020 for Thailand and end of January for the other three countries).[14] In Indonesia, the wage subsidy program was announced in early August 2020, and implementation began at the end of the month, approximately 6 months after the first COVID-19 case in the country was identified in early March 2020.[15] In general, the use of electronic transfers into personal bank accounts expedited the timely and quick payout of wage subsidies in all our sample countries. In the case of the Philippines (for the Small Business Wage Subsidy Program), this payment delivery method was also supplemented by the use of electronic vouchers or payment cards, and manual cash payments when other methods could not be used.

In general, labor market policies had limited coverage of the workforce, with the highest (in terms of targeted percentage of the workforce) afforded by Thailand's Rao Mai Ting Kan (Informal Workers Subsidy) Program (37%), and Malaysia's Employment Retention Program (24%). The adequacy of benefits was generally higher for the more targeted policies, with 75% of average wages for frontline health workers in the Philippines, and 62% of average wages for frontline education workers. In Viet Nam, the allowance for workers engaged in COVID-19 prevention and control exceeded average wages by 37%.

---

[13] Authors' calculations based on the Philippine Statistics Authority. 2019 Survey on Overseas Filipinos. https://psa.gov.ph/statistics/survey/labor-and-employment/survey-overseas-filipinos (accessed 12 August 2021).

[14] The "first COVID-19 case" is only one of the three proxy "triggers" used in Beazley, Marzi, and Stellar (2021). The other two triggers being the date when the pandemic was declared on 11 March 2020 ("pandemic declaration date") and the day that containment measures were implemented in each country ("stay home" date). The latter trigger in particular may be the most relevant as it marks the date that labor market impacts intensified in Southeast Asia. This will be considered in the next stage of our research.

[15] The exact "first COVID-19 cases" dates are 2 March 2020 in Indonesia, 26 January 2020 in Malaysia, 30 January 2020 in the Philippines, 13 January 2020 in Thailand, and 24 January 2020 in Viet Nam.

Social assistance

While job and income losses affected all households, the impacts are more likely to inflict scars on poor households. This is because poor households have lower savings and are more likely to have to sell productive assets, suffer food insecurity and schooling losses for children, with long-term consequences in terms of human capital and future income (World Bank 2021c). This points to a critical role for social assistance measures to compensate for income losses and sustain livelihoods. These measures constituted the largest component of the social protection response to COVID-19 in Southeast Asia. In this comparative analysis, we focus on the first and largest social assistance instrument used in Southeast Asia in response to the pandemic: emergency cash and in-kind transfers.

All countries in our sample implemented emergency cash transfers in response to COVID-19. In most cases, these interventions were built upon existing programs in these countries. However, in addition to these interventions, new measures, unrelated to existing programs were introduced in the Philippines, Indonesia, and Malaysia. Whether the interventions were linked to existing programs or not, in most cases, social registries or beneficiary databases from existing programs were used to rapidly identify beneficiaries. In a few cases, open registration or new enrollment campaigns were also used (for demand-based and community-based targeting). Disbursements were largely made through electronic transfers into personal bank accounts, and through electronic vouchers or payment cards, or both methods. In Indonesia and in the Philippines, these methods were supplemented by manual cash payments as needed.

In Indonesia, 81% of households reported a decrease in income in February–April 2020 compared with the same period in 2019 (Figure 3.7). Two emergency cash transfer measures and one in-kind transfer measure, building upon existing social assistance programs, were implemented from March to April 2020. The flagship Family Hope Program expanded its coverage and increased the level of benefits disbursed, and distributed the benefit monthly instead of quarterly. The 9 million existing beneficiaries (approximately 3.4% of the population) received a benefit top-up of 25%–56%, and coverage is estimated to have increased by 800,000 new beneficiaries. Through the BLT Village Fund Cash Assistance Program, a cash transfer was provided for 3 months initially and then extended for another 3 months, to poor persons living in rural areas and villages, primarily farmers and low-income families who have not received other government assistance. By June 2020, approximately 6.9 million beneficiaries had been observed, and the targeted/projected number of beneficiaries stood at 12.3 million. The Staple Food Card Program also expanded coverage and increased its transfer amount. Existing beneficiaries (15.2 million or 5.6% of the population) received an increase in transfer of 25%–36% and were joined by an additional 4.8 million recipients. Smaller-scale emergency cash and in-kind transfers were also made by the National Zakat Agency (BAZNAS), covering some 190,000 recipients. These programs were complemented with public works (cash for work) programs, targeting low-skilled workers (e.g., rural infrastructure development programs), informal workers, unemployed and underemployed persons, and marginalized communities.

Among the sample countries, Malaysia experienced the least severe impacts of the pandemic between February and April 2020, with just over half (54%) of survey respondents reporting a decline in income compared with the same period in 2019 (Figure 3.7). Nevertheless, in response to COVID-19, the Bantuan Sara Hidup Program's coverage of 4.3 million beneficiaries or 52% of the population, was expanded by 1.2 million, its benefits increased by 15%, and the disbursement was anticipated from May to March 2020. This intervention was accompanied by additional new policy measures, such as the Bantuan Prihatin Nasional, which gave a one-off cash transfer to its

10.6 million beneficiaries or one-third of the population (as of September 2020). Bantuan Prihatin Nasional beneficiaries included those with Bantuan Sara Hidup accounts and other low-income households or individuals aged 21 years or older. Payments were made in April and May 2020, with a second round of payments starting in October 2020. Additional cash transfers in Malaysia targeted vulnerable groups, including people with disabilities, single mothers, senior citizens, children in shelters, homeless persons, and indigenous persons.

Figure 3.7: Poverty Headcount Ratio, Declines in Household Incomes and Coverage Expansion of Social Assistance Programs in Response to COVID-19

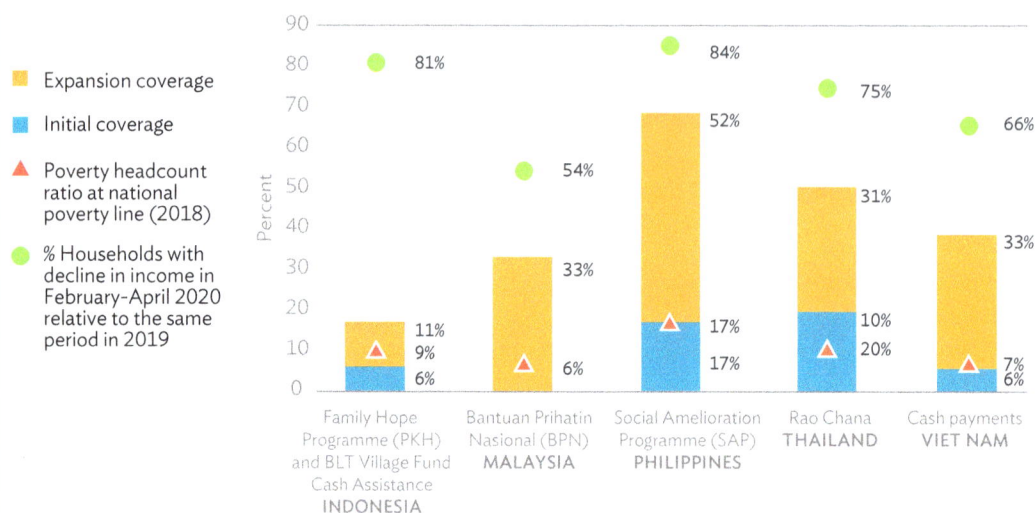

Sources: Authors' illustration based on International Policy Centre for Inclusive Growth. Social Protection Responses to COVID-19 in the Global South: Online Dashboard. https://socialprotection.org/social-protection-responses-covid-19-global-south (accessed 28 May 2021); World Bank. World Development Indicators. https://databank.worldbank.org/source/world-development-indicators (accessed 2 December 2021); and calculations using ADBI household Surveys in ASEAN countries.

Figure 3.8: Adequacy of Benefits for Large-Scale Emergency Cash Transfers

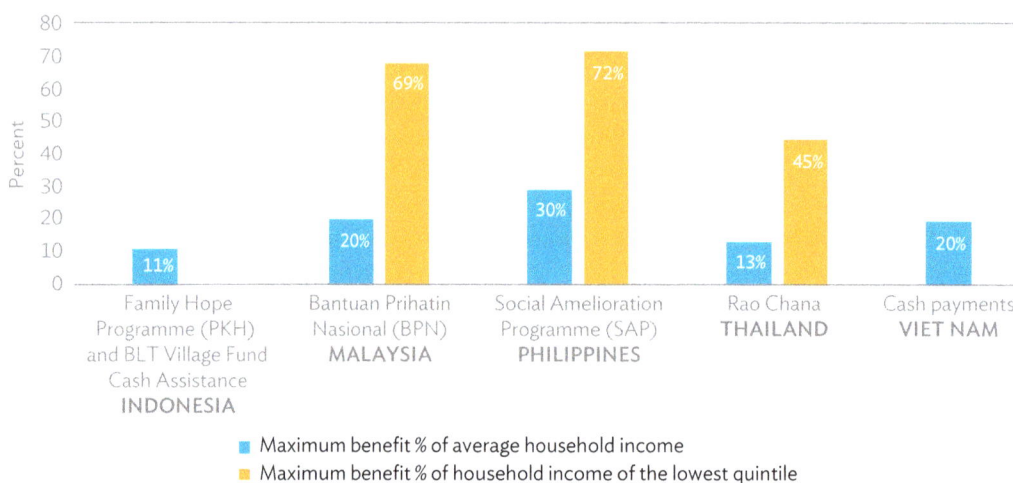

Source: International Policy Centre for Inclusive Growth. Social Protection Responses to COVID-19 in the Global South: Online Dashboard. https://socialprotection.org/social-protection-responses-covid-19-global-south (accessed 28 May 2021).

The Philippines had the largest share of households (84%) experiencing income losses in February–April 2020 compared with the same period in 2019. Its social assistance response to COVID-19, the Social Amelioration Program (SAP), was linked to the existing Pantawid Pamilyang Pilipino Program (4Ps) and the Rice Subsidy Program, which had approximately 4.4 million active household beneficiaries (approximately 17% of the population) in 2015. SAP targeted its coverage to expand to 13.3 million low-income families (52% of the population) in addition to the beneficiaries of the 4Ps program. The benefit amount of 4Ps recipients increased by twofold or even threefold. SAP had the highest adequacy of benefits among large-scale cash transfer programs implemented in the region, with a maximum benefit reaching 72% of the household income of the lowest income quintile (Figure 3.8). Additionally, an emergency subsidy program was introduced, to provide a one-time cash grant and food packs to households identified by their local government units as low income, but who did not qualify for benefits under SAP. In addition to social assistance programs, the Philippines also implemented a public works program for informal workers affected by the crisis, which included displaced, underemployed, and seasonal workers.

In Thailand, despite the crisis' relatively less severe effect on the labor market in the first half of 2020, 75% of survey respondents reported a decline in household income (Figure 3.7). In May 2020, approximately 13.4 million welfare card holders (unemployed or low-income individuals) or approximately 19% of the population, had their benefits increase by 56%. However, the more substantial expansion of the program was put into effect in 2021. Welfare card holders, who had increased to 13.7 million, saw a 338% increase in benefits, and the program and budget was expanded to cover an additional 21.5 million beneficiaries (out of whom 16.8 million had registered by April 2021).

In Viet Nam, two-thirds of respondents reported a decline in household income over February–April 2020 compared with the previous year (Figure 3.7). In response to COVID-19, social assistance measures primarily involved the expansion in April 2020 of existing cash transfer programs (covering 1.4 million persons with meritorious service[16] and recipients of other social protection programs) to approximately 10 million beneficiaries. The additional 8.6 million recipients (approximately 33% of the population) include those living in poor and near-poor households based on the national poverty line; unemployed persons or those with terminated employment contracts but are not eligible for unemployment benefits; self-employed workers who have lost their jobs; and household businesses with low revenues and had to temporarily suspend their business. The target group of this intervention therefore includes the large share of contributing family workers who exited the labor force as a result of the suspension of family business operations, as reflected in the overwhelming share of transitions out of the labor force (among the transitions out of employment) in Viet Nam in Q2 2020.

In addition to emergency cash and in-kind transfers, other social assistance measures carried out across Southeast Asia included subsidies for utilities, telecommunications, housing, loans/credit, and tuition. Two countries (Malaysia and the Philippines) expanded coverage of noncontributory health insurance. Some countries (Malaysia and the Philippines) implemented public work programs (cash for work), targeting low-skilled workers affected by the pandemic.

---

[16] Includes people who participated in the revolution, martyrs, Vietnamese heroic mothers, war invalids, etc.

Social insurance

Social insurance, the smaller component of social protection systems in Southeast Asia, also had a small contribution to the region's social protection response to COVID-19. Social insurance measures target formal workers, and therefore have minimal coverage in most of the region's economies. Social insurance interventions were generally linked to existing measures and covered four social protection areas: unemployment insurance, health insurance, sick leave and employment injury, and contributory pensions.

In Indonesia, social insurance interventions had to do mainly with health insurance. Specifically, low-income and vulnerable categories of workers (nonemployees and non-salaried employees) covered by the national health insurance scheme (JKN) and social security provider (BPJS Kesehatan) received subsidies for their health insurance premiums for a 6-month period. The premium (Rp42,000 per month, equivalent to $8.00 PPP) was paid to 96.6 million persons by the central government, and to 36 million others by the regional government. A Supreme Court decision also revoked a planned increase in health insurance premium for the most vulnerable insured workers.

In Malaysia, eligibility criteria for unemployment benefits under the Employment Insurance System (EIS) were relaxed for workers retrenched in COVID-19-affected sectors, claimable training costs were increased, and a daily training allowance was provided. In 2018, 7 million workers (44% of the labor force) were insured under the EIS. Among insured workers, just over 100,000 (0.6% of the labor force) had applied to benefit from this measure.

Another social insurance policy response in Malaysia allowed early withdrawals from the Employees Provident Fund, a pension fund based on voluntary contributions from employees, self-employed persons, and business owners. The fund covers 7.6 million workers (48% of the labor force), out of whom 3.5 million (22% of the labor force) had applied for early withdrawals by May 2020. Additionally, the government allowed early fund withdrawals for participants of the Private Retirement Scheme, amended the Employment Injury Scheme to cover accidents at home for workers with flexible work arrangements during the pandemic, and partially funded a work-injury scheme for employees in the gig economy.

In the Philippines, unemployment surged in Q2 2020 as strict containment measures affected displaced labor-absorbing sectors and prevented reallocation toward these sectors. Unemployment benefits were provided to premium-paying members of the Social Security System (SSS)[17] who lost their jobs due to layoffs or business closures or cessation of operations related to COVID-19, or due to illness or disease. The benefit amounts to half of the average monthly salary for a 2-month period. While the SSS had 18.4 million members (40% of the labor force) in 2018, enrollment for the unemployment benefit was demand-based and expected to cover between 30,000 and 60,000 workers (less than 1% of the labor force).

The Philippines also made changes to its PhilHealth contributory health insurance program, deferring the payment of contributions, waiving the 45-day coverage policy, and extending the filing period for claims. As a more targeted social insurance measure, the Philippines also provided one-off sickness and death cash benefits to public and private frontline workers who contracted

---

[17] Includes private sector employees, self-employed persons, and household workers, who must make mandatory payments, as well as voluntary contributors among Philippine citizens working abroad, persons who previously had mandatory coverage, and nonworking spouses of insured persons.

COVID-19 and who were insured by either the Government Social Insurance System or the SSS through the Employees' Compensation Program. As of December 2020, 4,000 workers had availed of these benefits.

In Thailand, most of the displaced workers in Q2 2020 (84%) had transitioned to unemployment, rather than out of the labor force. While the Rao Mai Ting Kan Program brought relief to informal workers, three new unemployment benefit measures were introduced, targeting formal workers: (i) "force majeure – unemployment benefits" for workers insured under the Social Security Fund affected by the crisis (for a duration of up to 3 months); (ii) "economic crisis – unemployment benefits" for insured workers during unemployed periods due to the crisis between March 2020 and February 2021 (for a duration of up to 7 months), and (iii) a one-off allowance for returning Thai migrant workers. Coverage of the "force majeure" policy was 984,000 or 2.5% of the labor force in May 2020, while just over 15,000 had received termination benefits under the "economic crisis" policy by March 2021.

In Viet Nam, health insurance policy coverage (87% of the population or approximately 84 million persons) was extended to cover COVID-19 patients, nationals or foreigners, and particularly targeting vulnerable persons including children, the elderly, the disabled, refugees, and internally displaced persons. As Viet Nam succeeded in containing the spread of the virus, only 1,500 persons needed this coverage by January 2021. Additionally, patients with chronic diseases were given medicines for at least 2 months at a time, and other administrative adjustments were made to ensure free health care was given to insurance cardholders, even during lockdowns or when medical facilities are exclusively treating COVID-19 patients.

In sum, the social insurance policy response to COVID-19 had limited reach in Southeast Asia, where coverage remains limited. Nevertheless, unemployment benefits and employment injury and sickness protection were extended to displaced formal workers who would not have been covered otherwise, including those who do not meet the eligibility criteria due to insufficient contributions, returning migrant workers, gig economy workers, and others.

Summary and Concluding Remarks

The COVID-19 pandemic hit Southeast Asia's economies hard, resulting in major job losses across many sectors. Job losses peaked in Q2 2020, when containment measures were most stringent. As mobility restrictions and workplace closures prevented labor reallocation across sectors and status-in-employment categories, unemployment surged in Indonesia, Malaysia, Thailand, and the Philippines. In Viet Nam, agricultural workers made up the largest share of job losses in Q2 2020 (specifically, contributing family work in agriculture), but the vast majority of job losses consisted of transitions out of the labor force. The massive drops in employment levels that took place in Q2 2020 understate the impact of the pandemic, however, because of major reductions in working hours for those employed.

The crisis had a differential effect on youth and on women. Young workers suffered a disproportionate amount of job losses, while women were more likely to exit the labor force following job loss than men. Exits from the labor force—particularly where female labor force participation is relatively low, as in the case of Indonesia and the Philippines—can have long-term adverse effects on the working lives of women. Although many female workers reentered the labor market in the second half of 2020, labor reallocation patterns indicate that part of the employment recovery consisted of "distress employment" or "added worker effect," suggesting that the quality of employment had taken a hit.

Informal workers and own-account workers, who make up a large segment of workers in highly affected sectors, were particularly vulnerable to the crisis. Informal workers suffered many job and income losses in the early stage of the pandemic, with self-employment as the most affected source of household income across Southeast Asia throughout 2020. As economies reopened and restrictions eased up in the second half of the year, employment picked up, but generally consisted of lower- quality jobs while the recovery of formal wage employment lagged behind that of informal employment and own-account work.

To counter the pandemic's devastating blow to jobs and incomes, governments around the world responded swiftly with significant fiscal and monetary measures. Fiscal response packages varied across countries in Southeast Asia, based on the severity of the pandemic's impact on jobs and incomes and available fiscal space. The amounts allocated to fiscal measures announced or implemented since the onset of the crisis ranged from 2.7% of GDP in Viet Nam to 18.8% of GDP in Thailand, with spending on social protection (health and income support measures) comprising around 65% of the response in Malaysia and Viet Nam, 77% in Thailand, 88% in the Philippines, and 91% in Indonesia. Although detailed data sets that allow the assessment of the effectiveness of policies in protecting jobs and incomes are not yet available for these countries, this report made an initial assessment of these policies in terms of their coverage, adequacy of benefits, and the extent to which they succeeded in reaching the most vulnerable and filling preexisting gaps. As additional data sources become available over time, a more rigorous assessment of these policy interventions will be possible.

Even before the pandemic, social protection was already weak in these countries, and support measures did not cover a large share of workers. Many of these workers, often informal, were neither covered by social insurance that targeted formal workers, nor social assistance that targeted the poorest and most vulnerable including children and others who are not employed.

Social assistance programs and particularly large-scale cash transfer programs played an integral role in these countries' social response. Key interventions consisted of massive horizontal expansion (or increased population coverage) of existing programs. In general, the use of electronic transfers into personal bank accounts and the existence of social registries and databases facilitated timely and speedy implementation of these interventions.

Social insurance measures may have benefited a small segment of formal workers, but their coverage remained lacking. The pandemic highlighted the vulnerability of informal workers to external shocks and their limited access to social protection, emphasizing the need for intensified formalization efforts.

Active labor market programs (ALMPs) including wage and training subsidies played an important role in each country's response. In general, labor market policies covered only a small number of the workforce, with the highest (in terms of targeted percentage of the workforce) afforded by Thailand's Informal Workers Subsidy Program and Malaysia's Employment Retention Program. The adequacy of benefits was generally higher for the more targeted policies. ALMPs, including policies for reskilling and upskilling, will continue to play a critical role in the future.

As technology, trade, and other megatrends continue to shape the region's labor markets, wider access to skills development and training will remain crucial to help transition displaced workers avail of decent work opportunities.

All countries in our sample have made attempts to fill some social protection gaps exposed by the crisis, by extending social protection to vulnerable groups. For instance, Thailand's labor market policy response targeted two broad vulnerable groups: informal workers and young workers. In the Philippines, a program targeted registered overseas Filipino workers (OFWs affected by the pandemic, who either remained abroad or were repatriated. In Indonesia, returning migrant workers were eligible for the pre-employment card program. In Malaysia, the government reduced the foreign worker levy for all companies that formally employed foreigners, to protect jobs, and extended unemployment benefits and employment injury and sickness to displaced formal workers who would not have been covered otherwise, including those who do not meet the eligibility criteria due to insufficient contributions, returning migrant workers, gig economy workers, and others.

While recovery prospects in Southeast Asia seemed positive by the end of 2020, the devastating impact of the Delta wave of the virus in 2021 coupled with slow vaccination rollout has required further containment measures and has derailed or, at least, delayed recovery. The longer the pandemic persists, and the more protracted it proves to be, the more difficult it is for governments to sustain interventions. For economies to begin to recover, accelerated vaccination process is critical in the short term. As recovery sets in, fiscal policy can shift to focus more strongly from relief to stimulus, and from stimulus to structural investments toward sustained and inclusive growth.

The pandemic, along with the real risks it poses to the region, of slower long-term economic growth and increased inequalities, has emphasized the need for fiscal policy to play a more redistributive role in the region (World Bank 2021c). Fiscal policy must transcend its countercyclical role, through increased investment in social protection and its infrastructure.

A key challenge for Southeast Asian countries is to leverage achievements in responding to the pandemic (through the use of digital technology and e-banking, for instance) and channel efforts made to temporarily fill social protection gaps, toward building more comprehensive, inclusive, and sustainable social protection systems. Addressing this challenge must be a priority, not only to reduce vulnerability to shocks but also to mitigate widening inequalities in labor market outcomes and living standards across and within countries.

Appendix

Appendix A1: Calculation of Change in Working Hours

Variable	Definition
H_t	Total hours worked at time t
E_t	Employed population at time t
$AH_t = H_t/E_t$	Average hours worked at time t

(A) Hours lost due to job loss:

$$Hours\ lost\ due\ to\ job\ loss_t = \Delta E_t {}^* AH_{t-1}$$

(B) Hours lost in employment:

$$Hours\ lost\ in\ employment_t = E_t {}^* \Delta AH_t$$

(C) Total working hours lost = (A) + (B)

Total working hours lost (%) = (C) / H_{t-1}
Intensive margin of adjustment (%) = (B) / (C)
Extensive margin of adjustment (%) = (A) / (C)

Notes:
(1) The difference operator Δ applied to variable X at time t refers to the change in the variable compared with the previous quarter value. Thus, $\Delta X_t = X_t - X_{t-1}$.
(2) Hours worked refer to total hours worked in the main job.

Table A1.1: Change in Employment by Sector and Status, Q3 2020 versus Q2 2020

| | Q3 2020 versus Q2 2020 | | | |
	Wage and Salaried Workers	Employer	Own-Account Workers	Unpaid Family Workers
Philippines				
Agriculture	588	343	698	476
Mining and quarrying	77	2	10	0
Manufacturing	531	31	54	58
Utilities	27	0	0	0
Construction	1,235	5	-2	1
Wholesale and retail	558	65	1,367	443
Transport and storage	255	3	57	5
Accommodation and food service	-92	-4	86	55
Information and communication	45	0	-10	4
Financial and insurance	114	1	5	1
Real estate	16	0	37	1
Professional, scientific and technical	8	1	1	6
Administrative and support services	27	4	2	-1
Public administration	76	0	0	0
Education	47	-2	5	0
Human health and social work	79	-1	5	1
Other services	9	3	52	2
Net change in the number of employed ('000s)	3,599	452	2,369	1,051
Status share in job gains (%)*	48%	6%	32%	14%
Thailand				
Agriculture	-60	-7	414	735
Mining and quarrying	0	0	1	-1
Manufacturing	-192	-4	-45	-11
Utilities	1	2	-1	0
Construction	-70	16	-15	28
Wholesale and retail	63	11	-25	8
Transport and storage	33	5	11	7
Accommodation and food service	24	-1	-2	59
Information and communication	-25	-5	1	0
Financial and insurance	18	0	1	0
Real estate	5	-1	1	1
Professional, scientific and technical	-10	-2	-1	-2
Administrative and support services	7	-5	12	3
Public administration	-31	0	0	0
Education	-56	1	3	2
Human health and social work	11	-2	0	-1
Other services	-59	0	1	3
Net change in the number of employed ('000s)	-341	9	354	831
Status share in job gains (%)*		1%	30%	70%

continued on next page

Table A1.1 continued

	Q3 2020 versus Q2 2020			
	Wage and Salaried Workers	**Employer**	**Own-Account Workers**	**Unpaid Family Workers**
Viet Nam				
Agriculture	103	7	655	-508
Mining and quarrying	6	2	4	0
Manufacturing	341	-29	105	-47
Utilities	-9	-4	-3	-2
Construction	252	-13	-3	-4
Wholesale and retail	117	-12	311	-97
Transport and storage	-51	-12	34	-1
Accommodation and food service	122	-5	-7	-31
Information and communication	11	0	-1	3
Financial and insurance	-24	-1	-3	-3
Real estate	-1	5	29	-2
Professional, scientific and technical	1	-1	3	3
Administrative and support services	16	2	13	-4
Public administration	37	0	-1	0
Education	77	6	-2	2
Human health and social work	26	8	8	2
Other services	46	-3	53	-9
Net change in the number of employed ('000s)	1,071	-51	1,194	-697
Status share in job gains (%)*	47%		53%	
Indonesia**				
Agriculture	-769	-13	688	647
Mining and quarrying	55	-6	-38	-15
Manufacturing	353	90	20	-122
Utilities	177	17	248	28
Construction	6,810	334	273	23
Wholesale and retail	-151	888	12,279	4,079
Transport and storage	-4,180	-1,023	-10,300	-3,892
Accommodation and food service	-699	294	2,083	1,897
Information and communication	-1,302	-285	-4,175	-1,697
Financial and insurance	824	-25	-188	-31
Real estate	-1,212	2	121	2
Professional, scientific and technical Administrative and support services	-254	43	-79	-8
Public administration	88	0	0	0
Education	421	-3	42	4
Human health and social work	253	16	33	0
Other services	-22	17	6	-54
Net change in the number of employed ('000s)	390	347	1,012	861
Status share in job gains (%)*	15%	13%	39%	33%

continued on next page

Table A1.1 continued

	Q4 2020 vs. Q3 2020			
	Wage and Salaried Workers	**Employer**	**Own-Account Workers**	**Unpaid Family Workers**
Philippines				
Agriculture	-295	174	-235	-750
Mining and quarrying	-55	-2	-30	-1
Manufacturing	-291	4	-7	-50
Utilities	4	0	1	0
Construction	-68	6	4	1
Wholesale and retail	-39	11	-117	-363
Transport and storage	-88	-6	10	-5
Accommodation and food service	103	28	-46	-22
Information and communication	149	6	-3	-5
Financial and insurance	47	0	-2	-2
Real estate	-12	0	-28	-1
Professional, scientific and technical	58	-1	-11	-6
Administrative and support ser	191	-2	9	1
Public administration	-131	0	0	0
Education	262	1	6	0
Human health and social work	37	7	12	-1
Other services	76	2	-1	0
Net change in the number of employed ('000s)	-52	229	-438	-1,204
Status share in job gains (%)*		100%		
Thailand				
Agriculture	159	6	-11	-279
Mining and quarrying	51	1	6	1
Manufacturing	85	6	32	34
Utilities	42	1	8	3
Construction	125	-15	9	-27
Wholesale and retail	36	1	-4	25
Transport and storage	-10	-4	5	-3
Accommodation and food service	-25	15	42	-4
Information and communication	-6	2	2	2
Financial and insurance	-9	3	7	2
Real estate	14	8	13	0
Professional, scientific and technical	-1	4	24	9
Administrative and support services	-15	3	2	-4
Public administration	-24	0	0	0
Education	8	-1	-2	-1
Human health and social work	38	-2	14	1
Other services	-6	8	-35	-4
Net change in the number of employed ('000s)	461	37	112	-246
Status share in job gains (%)*	76%	6%	18%	

continued on next page

Table A1.1 continued

	Q4 2020 vs. Q3 2020			
	Wage and Salaried Workers	**Employer**	**Own-Account Workers**	**Unpaid Family Workers**
Viet Nam				
Agriculture	131	-23	-338	-20
Mining and quarrying	-5	0	-2	2
Manufacturing	349	-38	62	17
Utilities	8	0	7	3
Construction	57	16	-14	-2
Wholesale and retail	41	-44	13	-8
Transport and storage	99	11	58	0
Accommodation and food service	-13	-15	66	-4
Information and communication	1	0	1	0
Financial and insurance	46	-2	4	1
Real estate	20	-3	7	-2
Professional, scientific and technical	34	2	-2	-1
Administrative and support services	27	3	12	8
Public administration	-22	0	-1	1
Education	27	0	3	1
Human health and social work	-10	-8	-9	-2
Other services	66	4	-12	14
Net change in the number of employed ('000s)	858	-99	-144	8
Status share in job gains (%)*	1,584	-175	51	37

Q = quarter.
* Status in employment share is calculated over the sum of job gains (excluding sectors where net change in jobs was negative).
**Indonesia: Change refers to August 2020–February 2021.
Source: Authors' calculations based on labor force surveys.

Table A1.2: Correlation Matrix, Intensive Margins of Adjustment, and Related Variables at the Sectoral Level (2-Digit ISIC)

	Intensive Margins of Adjustment (%)	Teleworkability (%)	MSME Share (%)	Temporary Worker Share (%)	Wage Employment Share (%)	Low-Skilled Share (%)
Viet Nam						
Intensive margins of adjustment	1.000					
Teleworkability	-0.035	1.000				
MSME share	0.1755	-0.0024	1.000			
Temporary worker share	0.0524	-0.5833*	0.4195*	1.000		
Wage employment share	-0.1597	0.3038*	-0.6941*	-0.5749*	1.000	
Low-skilled share	-0.003	-0.3347*	0.3167*	0.4244*	-0.3827*	1.000
Philippines						
Intensive margins of adjustment	1.000					
Teleworkability	-0.1224	1.000				
Temporary worker share	-0.2659*	-0.3101*		1.000		
Wage employment share	-0.0226	0.3544*		0.1939	1.000	
Low-skilled share	0.0769	-0.4927*		0.3409*	-0.2555*	1.000
Thailand						
Intensive margins of adjustment	1.000					
Teleworkability	-0.1081	1.000				
MSME share	-0.0083	0.1012	1.000			
Wage employment share	-0.1838	0.2861*	-0.0526		1.000	
Low-skilled share	0.0251	-0.4078*	0.0234		-0.3473*	1.000

*Significant at the 5% level
ISIC = International Standard Industrial Classification, MSME = micro, small, and medium-sized enterprise
There are 88 2-digit ISIC sectors in the sample.
Notes:
(i) Intensive margins are calculated as per Appendix A1. Negative values are set to zero, values greater than 100% are set to 100.
(ii) Teleworkability indices are computed following Generalao (2021), derived by employing a task-based approach and classifying whether a task of an occupation is considered manual, requires physically assisting and caring for others or to be done outdoors, and can be effectively done with the aid of information and communication technology services and devices. The index is scaled from 0 to 1, wherein an occupation with a value of 1 implies that all tasks performed in the occupation can be done entirely at home or offsite, while a value of 0 suggests the opposite. An index value between 0 and 1 means that not all tasks of the particular occupation can be performed from home or offsite. See Generalao (2021) for the detailed task classification process and description of the indices.
(iii) Correlations could not be computed for Indonesia, for which employment data by economic activity are not available at the 2-digit ISIC level in the LFS, but only at the 1-digit level.
(iv) There is no data available for MSME share in employment in the Philippines and temporary employment in Thailand.
Source: Authors' estimates based on labor force surveys.

Table A2.1: Labor Market Indicators by Age and Sex Groups , Q4 2019–Q2 2021
(%)

Period	Age	Sex	Indonesia* EPR	Indonesia* UR	Indonesia* LFPR	Malaysia EPR	Malaysia UR	Malaysia LFPR	Philippines EPR	Philippines UR	Philippines LFPR	Thailand EPR	Thailand UR	Thailand LFPR	Viet Nam EPR	Viet Nam UR	Viet Nam LFPR
Q4 2019	15–24	Male	46.3	18.4	56.7	48.3	8.8	52.9	39.2	12.1	44.6	46.3	4.4	48.4	55.0	6.7	58.9
		Female	32.0	19.0	39.5	33.8	11.6	38.3	24.9	14.1	29.0	32.2	6.2	34.3	50.2	6.3	53.5
		Total	39.3	18.6	48.3	41.4	9.9	45.9	32.3	12.8	37.0	39.3	5.1	41.4	52.7	6.5	56.3
	25 and over	Male	88.3	2.9	90.9	89.9	1.9	91.6	84.0	3.1	86.7	80.8	0.6	81.3	84.6	1.3	85.7
		Female	54.0	2.5	55.3	61.5	1.7	62.6	53.1	2.7	54.6	63.1	0.4	63.4	73.7	1.3	74.7
		Total	71.0	2.7	73.0	76.2	1.8	77.6	68.5	2.9	70.5	71.6	0.5	71.9	79.0	1.3	80.1
Q1 2020	15–24	Male	48.1	16.7	57.8	44.6	10.6	49.9	38.9	13.5	45.0	44.1	4.9	46.4	54.3	6.4	58.0
		Female	33.0	15.6	39.2	31.8	11.7	36.0	25.4	14.0	29.5	32.3	5.3	34.1	48.0	7.8	52.0
		Total	40.8	16.3	48.7	38.5	11.0	43.3	32.3	13.6	37.4	38.3	5.1	40.3	51.2	7.0	55.1
	25 and over	Male	88.7	3.1	91.5	90.4	2.0	92.2	83.0	3.9	86.4	81.0	0.7	81.6	84.2	1.2	85.2
		Female	57.3	2.6	58.8	61.7	1.8	62.9	53.6	3.3	55.4	63.6	0.5	64.0	71.7	1.4	72.7
		Total	72.9	2.9	75.0	76.5	1.9	78.1	68.2	3.7	70.8	71.9	0.6	72.3	77.8	1.3	78.8
Q2 2020	15–24	Male				42.8	12.6	49.0	27.8	30.7	40.1	44.5	7.9	48.3	52.9	7.1	57.0
		Female				31.5	12.3	35.9	16.4	32.8	24.4	29.4	9.9	32.6	46.2	6.9	49.6
		Total				37.4	12.5	42.8	22.2	31.5	32.4	37.0	8.7	40.5	49.7	7.0	53.4
	25 and over	Male				88.7	3.2	91.6	67.7	16.5	81.2	80.7	1.3	81.7	79.7	1.9	81.2
		Female				59.3	4.1	61.8	41.8	12.5	47.8	62.7	1.2	63.4	67.5	2.1	68.9
		Total				74.5	3.6	77.3	54.7	15.0	64.4	71.3	1.2	72.1	73.4	2.0	74.9
Q3 2020	15–24	Male	44.7	20.8	56.4	44.0	11.7	49.9	37.8	19.8	47.1	44.4	7.4	48.0	51.9	5.7	55.0
		Female	32.5	19.9	40.6	28.5	13.9	33.1	22.3	26.5	30.3	30.6	9.4	33.8	45.4	9.1	50.0
		Total	38.6	20.5	48.6	36.6	12.6	41.8	30.2	22.4	38.9	37.6	8.2	41.0	48.8	7.2	52.6
	25 and over	Male	85.1	5.1	89.7	88.6	3.4	91.7	79.2	7.9	86.0	81.3	1.3	82.4	82.4	1.3	83.5
		Female	54.4	3.8	56.5	61.3	2.9	63.2	51.4	6.7	55.0	64.2	1.2	65.0	69.3	2.2	70.8
		Total	69.7	4.6	73.1	75.5	3.2	77.9	65.2	7.4	70.5	72.4	1.2	73.3	75.6	1.7	76.9

continued on next page

Table A2.1 continued

			Indonesia*			Malaysia			Philippines			Thailand			Viet Nam		
			EPR	UR	LFPR	EPR	UR	LFPR	EPR	UR	LFPR	EPR	UR	LFPR	EPR	UR	LFPR
Q4 2020	15–24	Male				45.0	11.4	50.7	33.3	18.7	40.9	47.0	7.1	50.5	49.7	5.2	52.4
		Female				28.4	15.1	33.4	21.1	20.6	26.6	32.7	8.1	35.6	44.4	9.2	48.8
		Total				37.0	12.8	42.4	27.3	19.4	33.9	39.9	7.5	43.2	47.1	7.1	50.7
	25 and over	Male				88.3	3.5	91.4	78.5	6.8	84.2	81.5	1.2	82.5	83.6	1.1	84.5
		Female				61.3	2.8	63.1	48.2	6.7	51.6	64.5	1.2	65.3	70.3	2.1	71.8
		Total				75.3	3.2	77.8	63.3	6.8	67.9	72.6	1.2	73.5	76.7	1.6	78.0
Q1 2021	15–24	Male	44.8	19.3	55.5	45.9	11.9	52.1				43.4	6.1	46.2	44.3	7.4	47.8
		Female	33.9	16.2	40.5	29.2	12.4	33.3				30.5	7.5	33.0	38.5	6.9	41.4
		Total	39.4	18.0	48.1	37.9	12.1	43.2				37.0	6.7	39.7	41.5	7.2	44.7
	25 and over	Male	85.4	4.7	89.5	88.3	3.3	91.3				80.1	0.9	80.9	78.8	1.7	80.2
		Female	55.7	3.4	57.7	60.8	3.6	63.0				63.6	0.8	64.1	65.2	1.3	66.1
		Total	70.5	4.2	73.6	75.0	3.4	77.6				71.5	0.9	72.1	71.7	1.5	72.8
Q2 2021	15–24	Male													42.7	7.2	46.0
		Female													37.0	7.7	40.1
		Total													39.9	7.4	43.1
	25 and over	Male													79.0	1.8	80.5
		Female													64.7	1.9	66.0
		Total													71.6	1.8	72.9

EPR = employment-to-population ratio, LFPR = labor force participation rate, Q = quarter, UR = unemployment rate.
*Indonesia Q4 2019 is August 2019; Q1 2020 is February 2020; Q3 2020 is August 2020; and Q1 2021 is February 2021.
Note: The working population in Malaysia is 15–64 years old; in other countries, it is 15+ years old.
Sources: Labor force surveys of various countries; International Labour Organization. ILOSTAT. Short-Term Labour Force Statistics (STLFS). https://ilostat.ilo.org/data/ (accessed 26 November 2021).

Table A3.1: Selected Labor Market and Employment Protection Policy Responses to COVID-19

		Timeliness		Coverage			Adequacy	Budget/ Cost/ Funding Source
	Short Description	Date Announced	Date Implemented	Eligibility (Target Group / Fills social protection gap?)	Number of Beneficiaries	% Labor Force	Benefit Amount	
Indonesia								
Wage Subsidy Program for Workers[a]	Active social security members with earnings of less than Rp5 million per month to receive wage subsidies for 4 months	4 Aug 2020	27 Aug 2020	• Active members of the BPJS with income of less than Rp5 million per month • Contract workers, teachers, firefighters, hotel workers, nurses, and cleaning staff (except for civil servants in these categories)	11,900,000	8.7%	• Bimonthly wage subsidy of Rp1,200,000 (Rp600,000 or $114.70 PPP per month) • Maximum monthly benefit amount as share of GDP per capita: 12% • Benefit percentage of average wage: 20.6%	Rp37.7 trillion/ State budget
Preemployment Card Program	• Cash for training or other job incentives (ALMP) • Requires online registration	25 Feb 2020	9 Apr 2020	• Indonesian citizens aged 18 years or older not currently attending formal education • Workers affected by layoffs, workers in the tourism sector, workers in micro or small sectors affected by the COVID-19 crisis, and workers who need job skills development • Indonesian returning migrant workers from Malaysia, Singapore, and Hong Kong, China	5,600,000	4.1%	• Rp600,000 ($114.70 PPP) per month for completing training course and Rp150,000 ($28.68 PPP) for completing three evaluation surveys. [5] • Maximum monthly benefit amount as share of GDP per capita: 12% • Benefit percentage of average wage: 20.6%	Rp20 trillion/ National economic recovery budget

continued on next page

Table A3.1 continued

	Short Description	Timeliness		Coverage			Adequacy	Budget/Cost/Funding Source
		Date Announced	Date Implemented	Eligibility (Target Group/Fills social protection gap?)	Number of Beneficiaries	% Labor Force	Benefit Amount	
Wage Subsidy Program for Educational Personnel	Wage subsidy program to support frontline workers in education	17 Nov 2020	1 Nov 2020	• Indonesian citizens, non–civil servants, with income below Rp5 million per month, are not a beneficiary of the Wage Subsidy Program of the Ministry of Manpower, not a beneficiary of the preemployment card as of 1 Oct 2020	1,999,000	1.5%	• Rp1,800,000 per month ($344 PPP) • Maximum monthly benefit amount as share of GDP per capita: 35.9% • Benefit percentage of average wage: 61.8%	Rp3,670,000
Safety Program by the National Police	Cash transfer to taxi, bus, and truck drivers	31 Mar 2020	15 Apr 2020	Taxi, bus, and/or truck drivers and bus driver assistants	197,000	0.14%	• Rp600,000 per month ($114.70 PPP) • Maximum monthly benefit amount as share of GDP per capita: 12%	Rp360 billion
Malaysia								
Wage Subsidy Program	Employment Retention Program: Subsidized wages of employees insured under the Social Security Organization (SOCSO) Employment Insurance Scheme (EIS) to assist employers in retaining their workers during the COVID-19 crisis	…	20 Mar 2020	• Phase 1: Employees earning RM4,000 or less who contribute to SOCSO's EIS, and whose employers are experiencing more than 50% decrease in their income since 1 Jan 2020, and do not retrench, impose unpaid leave, or force a wage cut on their employees from the start of the subsidy	3,940,000	24.7%	• RM600 (PPP $353.82) a month per worker to firms with more than 200 employees • RM800 ($471.76 PPP) a month per worker to firms with 76–200 employees • RM1,200 ($707.64 PPP) a month per worker to firms with less than 76 employees	Phase 1: RM5.9 billion; Phase 2: RM2.4 billion/ Part of second stimulus package of RM25 billion (1.7% of GDP)

continued on next page

Table A3.1 continued

Short Description	Timeliness		Coverage			Adequacy	Budget/Cost/Funding Source
	Date Announced	Date Implemented	Eligibility (Target Group/Fills social protection gap?)	Number of Beneficiaries	% Labor Force	Benefit Amount	
			Phase 2: Employees earning RM4,000 or less who contribute to SOCSO's EIS and whose employers are still affected by the pandemic, and who since the Recovery Movement Control Order are still facing lower revenues of at least 30% compared with 2019; companies registered with the SOCSO before 1 Sep 2020 and registered with the Companies Commission Malaysia or the relevant local authority before 1 Sep 2020 • Employers are forbidden to retrench workers earning RM4,000 or less but can reduce working hours or wages if their workers agree after a negotiation			• Maximum monthly benefit amount as share of GDP per capita: 15.5% • Benefit share of average wage: 38.6%	
Special Allowance to Frontline Workers	Health care and other frontline workers to receive a monthly allowance until the end of the COVID-19 outbreak	27 Feb 2020	1 Mar 2020	Doctors and other medical personnel, frontline personnel like immigration officers at entry points directly involved in the management and containment of the outbreak	17,000	0.11%	• Initially RM400 and RM200 ($235.88 PPP and $117.94) to doctors and other medical personnel and frontline personnel, respectively	Not available

continued on next page

Table A3.1 continued

Short Description	Timeliness		Coverage			Adequacy	Budget/Cost/Funding Source
	Date Announced	Date Implemented	Eligibility (Target Group/Fills social protection gap?)	Number of Beneficiaries	% Labor Force	Benefit Amount	
						• Later increased to RM600 to health-care personnel and RM400 to the other categories ($353.81 PPP and $235.88 PPP, respectively) • Maximum monthly benefit amount as share of GDP per capita: 15.5% • Benefit share of average wage: 11.5%	
Childcare subsidy	A new program to support working parents of young children through the subsidy of childcare expenses	5 Jun 2020	1 Jun 2020	Households with young children and working parents	5,000	Not available	• eVouchers of RM800 ($471.76 PPP) per household for mobile childcare services, and increase in income tax relief for parents on childcare services expenses • Maximum monthly benefit amount as share of GDP per capita: 20.6% • Benefit share of average wage: 25.9%	RM200 million

continued on next page

Table A3.1 continued

Short Description	Timeliness		Coverage			Adequacy	Budget/Cost/Funding Source
	Date Announced	Date Implemented	Eligibility (Target Group/Fills social protection gap?)	Number of Beneficiaries	% Labor Force	Benefit Amount	
Hiring and Training Assistance for Businesses	5 Jun 2020	31 Aug 2020	Employers must be registered under the SSM or other authorities and SOCSO before 1 Jun 2020 Applications for the incentives are based on the employee list within that registration • Youth: school leavers and graduates • Unemployed persons: all ages or with disabilities • Non-eligible are the following: (i) employees currently receiving Employment Retention Program assistance, (ii) listed in the Subsidy Program Wages; (iii) those who resign voluntarily; (iv) internship students who have not yet completed their employment; (v) parents, spouses, siblings or children taken as employees; (vi) employees who once worked and were recruited to work with the same employer	300,000	1.9%	• RM600 to RM1,000 ($353.82 PPP to $589.70) of monthly allowance and RM4,000 ($2,358.80 PPP) as a one-off training allowance • Maximum monthly benefit amount as share of GDP per capita: 25.8% • Benefit share of average wage: 32.4%	RM1.5 billion
Philippines							
COVID-19 Adjustment Measures Program (CAMP) Cash aid for affected workers of private establishments that implemented flexible work arrangements or suspended business operations due to the pandemic	17 Mar 2020	20 Mar 2020	Workers of private establishments that implemented flexible work arrangements or suspended business operations (temporary closure) due to the pandemic	657,201	1.4%	• ₱5,000 ($248.52 PPP) • Maximum monthly benefit amount as share of GDP per capita: 34.7% • Benefit share of average wage: 34.0%	₱3.286 billion

continued on next page

Table A3.1 continued

	Short Description	Timeliness — Date Announced	Timeliness — Date Implemented	Coverage — Eligibility (Target Group/Fills social protection gap?)	Coverage — Number of Beneficiaries	Coverage — % Labor Force	Adequacy — Benefit Amount	Budget/Cost/Funding Source
COVID-19 Hazard Pay	Hazard pay for public health workers serving in the frontlines	23 Mar 2020	17 Mar 2020	• Personnel who physically report for work during the implementation of an enhanced community quarantine (ECQ) • Personnel occupying regular, contractual, or casual positions; those engaged through contract of service, job order, or other similar schemes	703	0.002%	• ₱500 per day or ₱11,000 per month (22 working days). Equivalent $546.74 PPP • Maximum monthly benefit amount as share of GDP per capita: 76.3% • Benefit share of average wage: 74.9%	₱15 million / Department of Health (DOH)
Small Business Wage Subsidy	Wage subsidy to employees in small businesses affected by the ECQ	14 Apr 2020	1 May 2020	• Small businesses[b] under both Category A (non-essentials) and Category B (quasi-essentials) can apply for the wage subsidy for employees who did not work and did not get paid during the ECQ • Employees who fulfill all of the following criteria are eligible: (i) employee of an eligible small business; (ii) employed and active as of 1 Mar 2020 but unable to work due to the ECQ; (iii) did not get paid by their employer for at least 2 weeks during the temporary closure or suspension of work under Labor Advisory No. 1, Series of 2020; (iv) of any contract status (e.g., regular, probationary, regular seasonal, project-based, fixed-term); (v) certified by the employer in the application as having met all the above criteria	3,400,000	7.4%	• ₱5,000 to ₱8,000 ($248 to $397 PPP) • Maximum monthly benefit amount as share of GDP per capita: 55.5% • Benefit share of average wage: 54.5%	₱50.8 billion / Bayanihan 1

continued on next page

Table A3.1 continued

	Short Description	Timeliness		Coverage			Adequacy	Budget/Cost/Funding Source
		Date Announced	Date Implemented	Eligibility (Target Group/Fills social protection gap?)	Number of Beneficiaries	% Labor Force	Benefit Amount	
COVID-19 Special Risk Allowance	Allowance for workers providing care to COVID-19 patients	25 Mar 2020	1 Feb 2020	• Public and private health workers directly catering to or in contact with COVID-19 patients[c] • Private health workers assigned in the designated COVID-19 units of hospitals, laboratories, or medical and quarantine facilities as certified by the Department of Health	…	…	₱5,000	Part of ₱13.5 billion appropriated under Section 10a of RA No. 11494 for health-related responses to COVID-19
Thailand								
Rao Mai Ting Kan	Informal workers not insured under the Social Security Fund (SSF) can apply to receive a cash transfer for 3 months during the State of Emergency	25 Mar 2020	1 Apr 2020	• Thai informal workers: temporary, contractors, or self-employed workers	14,500,000	37.1%	• B5,000 ($388.40 PPP) • Maximum monthly benefit amount as share of GDP per capita: 24.1% • Benefit share of average wage: 32.9%	Part of B200 billion stimulus measure approved by cabinet 24 Mar 2020
Subsidies to Salaries of New Graduates	Wage subsidies to new graduates in companies insured under the SSF	8 Sep 2020	31 Oct 2020	New graduates from universities and vocational colleges not older than 25 years old, unless they graduated in 2019 or 2020 Companies entitled to participate in the program must be in the social security system and must not lay off more than 15% of their staff during the 1-year period	260,000	0.7%		B23.48 billion / Loan from the Ministry of Finance

continued on next page

Table A3.1 continued

Short Description	Timeliness		Coverage			Adequacy	Budget/ Cost/ Funding Source
	Date Announced	Date Implemented	Eligibility (Target Group/Fills social protection gap?)	Number of Beneficiaries	% Labor Force	Benefit Amount	
						• Salaries set at B15,000 for university graduates, B11,500 for graduates with advanced vocational certificates, and B9,400 for graduates with standard vocational certificates • The government to pay 50% of salaries for new graduates during the 1-year period (Equivalent $582.60 to $365.10 PPP) • Maximum monthly benefit amount as share of GDP per capita: 72.2% • Benefit share of average wage: 49.3%	

continued on next page

Table A3.1 continued

	Timeliness		Coverage			Adequacy	Budget/ Cost/ Funding Source
Short Description	Date Announced	Date Implemented	Eligibility (Target Group/Fills social protection gap?)	Number of Beneficiaries	% Labor Force	Benefit Amount	

Viet Nam

Unemployment Benefits							
3-month unemployment benefits to workers whose contract was suspended or who took unpaid leave	9 Apr 2020	9 Apr 2020	Workers whose employment contract was suspended or who took unpaid leave for at least 1 month because the employer lacks funds to pay wages due to COVID–19	Not available	Not available	• D1,800,000 ($224.39 PPP) • Maximum monthly benefit amount as share of GDP per capita: 33.9% • Benefit share of average wage: 2.0%	Part of stimulus package of D62 trillion
Anti-Epidemic Allowance Regime							
Allowance for workers involved in prevention and control of COVID–19	29 Mar 2020	29 Mar 2020	• Group 1: Persons who go to epidemic supervision, investigation and verification; people directly examining, diagnosing, and treating infected people at medical examination and treatment establishments • Group 2: Transporters of patients and medical products; preserving the patient's corpse; clothes washers, doctors, patients; collection of chemical bottles, jars and boxes; protection of isolation treatment areas; cleaning, disinfecting and destroying pathogens in isolation areas at medical examination and treatment establishments; health workers performing epidemiological surveillance and medical monitoring at home; medical isolators and medical isolators as designated by state management agencies.	Not available	Not available	• Varies from D80,000 to D300,000 per day depending on the workers occupation. • D1,936,000 to D6,600,000 per month (22 working days), equivalent up to $1,137.52 PPP) • Maximum monthly benefit amount as share of GDP per capita: 124% • Benefit share of average wage: 137%	Part of the D6.7 trillion stage budget

continued on next page

Off due to budget

Table A3.1 continued

| Short Description | Timeliness | | Coverage | | | Adequacy | Budget/ |
	Date Announced	Date Implemented	Eligibility (Target Group/Fills social protection gap?)	Number of Beneficiaries	% Labor Force	Benefit Amount	Cost/ Funding Source
			• Group 3: Persons performing the tasks (not being medical professionals) at the concentrated isolation facility (not applicable to isolation at home, accommodation, hotel, resort, business); participants in the enforcement of medical isolation in case the isolation measure must be applied but fails to comply with the medical isolation measure; Interpreters, emergency team 115, quarantine crew • Group 4: participants who are always anti-epidemic 24/24 hours, namely medical staff, the military, the police, performing their duties at the concentrated medical isolation facility (not applicable to the isolation at home, accommodation, hotel, resort, enterprise); participants performing the task of diversifying and carrying out procedures for people entering; guardians of isolated areas in residential areas as designated by state management agencies; medical staff who are on duty 24/24 at medical isolation treatment facilities to take care of and treat sufferers and suspects of COVID-19 • Group 5: training regime for collaborators and volunteers participating in the fight against epidemics during the COVID-19 epidemic				

ALMP = active labor market program, GDP = gross domestic product, PPP = purchasing power parity, SSM = Companies Commission Malaysia.

a The first transfer reached only 2.5 million workers, and the government aimed to reach more than 15 million. The Ministry of Manpower, employers, and BPJS integrated members' account details to the BPJS account in less than a month. [3]

b The small business must not be in the BIR's Large Taxpayer Service list. Employers in areas where other forms of quarantine have been put in place by the local government may also qualify.

c These include civilian employees occupying regular, contractual, or casual positions, whether full or part-time; workers engaged though contract of service or job order, including duly accredited and registered barangay health workers, who are assigned to hospitals, laboratories or medical and quarantine facilities, and whose official duties and responsibilities are directly related to the health-care response of the government to COVID-19.

Source: International Policy Centre for Inclusive Growth. 2021 Social Protection Responses to COVID-19 in the Global South. Mapping table. https://socialprotection.org/social-protection-responses-covid-19-global-south (accessed 9 November 2021).

Table A3.2: Social Assistance – Large-Scale Emergency Cash and In-Kind Transfers

	Timeliness		Coverage			Adequacy	Budget/ Cost/ Funding Source
Short Description	Date Announced	Date Implemented	Eligibility (Target Group/Fills social protection gap?)	Number of Beneficiaries	% Population	Benefit Amount	
Indonesia							
Family Hope Program (PKH) (preexisting program)	31 Mar 2020	8 Apr 2020	• Targets poor households (HHs) with pregnant women, children, severely disabled persons, and/or elderly persons aged 70 years or older[a]	• Existing beneficiaries: 9,066,786 with additional 800,000 • Vertical expansion (VE) top-up for 9,066,786	3.4% plus 1.2%	• Regular assistance: Rp129,167 PPP (in constant 2017 dollars) $25 per month for every HH • Components (per month): Rp312,500 to pregnant women or children aged 0–6 years; Rp93,750 to children in elementary school; Rp156,250 to children in junior high school; Rp208,333 to children in senior high school; Rp250,000 to persons with severe disability or elderly persons aged 70 years or older • Each eligible family can receive a maximum of four benefits	Rp37.4 trillion/ Fiscal package

continued on next page

Coverage of the PKH, the flagship conditional cash transfer program, was increased, as were the level of benefits disbursed

Table A3.2 continued

Short Description	Timeliness		Coverage			Adequacy	Budget/ Cost/ Funding Source
	Date Announced	Date Implemented	Eligibility (Target Group/Fills social protection gap?)	Number of Beneficiaries	% Population	Benefit Amount	
						• Maximum benefit per month: Rp1,129,167.00 • Benefit as share of average HH income: 0.11 • Benefit as share of average HH consumption expenditure: 0.14 • VE: top-up of benefits: 25% to 56%	
BLT Village Fund Cash Assistance (preexisting program)	Cash transfer to low-income households that did not receive assistance from other programs[b]	18 Apr 2020	Could not be verified: disbursement made for April, May, June	Poor persons who live in the villages and have not received social assistance from programs amid the COVID-19 crisis	• 6,881,778 beneficiaries in June 2020 versus expected number of beneficiaries 12,347,000	2.5% to increase to 9.9%	• Rp600,000 from April to June and Rp300,000 from July to December. $114.70 PPP from April to June and $57.35 PPP from July to December • Benefit as share of average HH income: 0.11 • Benefit as share of average HH consumption expenditure: 0.14	Rp22,4 trillion / Village funds

continued on next page

Table A3.2 continued

Short Description	Timeliness		Coverage			Adequacy	Budget/Cost/Funding Source
	Date Announced	Date Implemented	Eligibility (Target Group/Fills social protection gap?)	Number of Beneficiaries	% Population	Benefit Amount	
Staple food card Increased coverage of food transfers[c]	8 Apr 2020 (preparing staple food for people across the country) 25 Mar 2020 (increasing the allowance from Rp150,000 to Rp200,000)	1 Mar 2020 1 Mar 2020	• Poorest 25% of households or with the lowest socioeconomic status • Card allows poor families to buy basic dietary items from electronic shops	• Existing: 15,200,000 • New: 4,800,000	5.6% expanded to 6.9%	• Rp200,000 ($38.23 PPP) Benefit as share of average household income: 0.02 • Benefit as share of average HH consumption expenditure: 0.03 • Benefit increased by 36%	Rp43.6 trillion / Fiscal package
Malaysia							
Bantuan Sara Hidup (BSH) (existing program) Coverage of the BSH increased to an additional 1.2 million households and previous beneficiaries received a top-up	27 Feb 2020 (First stimulus package, which includes BSH program) 27 Feb 2020 (vertical expansion)	31 Mar 2020 1 May 2020 (Date of payment)	• Household – married couple A. The applicant: Malaysian citizen. Resident in Malaysia. Monthly household income less than RM4,000. B. Spouse of applicant: Malaysian citizen. For non-Malaysian spouse must be resident and holder of MyPR/MyKAS.	• Existing: 4,300,000 (in 2019) • New: additional 1,200,000	52.5% (plus 14.6%)	• HHs earning below RM2,000/month: RM1,000 per year • HHs earning RM2,001–RM3,000/month: RM750/year • HHs earning RM3,001–RM4,000/month • Benefit as share of average HH income: 0.01	RM3.2 billion / Malaysian government

continued on next page

Table A3.2 continued

| Short Description | Timeliness | | Coverage | | | Adequacy | Budget/ Cost/ Funding Source |
	Date Announced	Date Implemented	Eligibility (Target Group/Fills social protection gap?)	Number of Beneficiaries	% Population	Benefit Amount	
Bantuan Prihatin Nasional (BPN) (new intervention)	• Cash transfer to middle-class workers and low-income households • In 2021, it was replaced by the Bantuan Prihatin Rakyat (BPR)	27 Mar 2020	30 Apr 2020	Low-income households or single individuals in the middle 40% of workers (middle-class) or the bottom 40% of earners (lower class)	10,600,000 as of 23 Sep 2020	33.2%	• RM1,600 to HHs earning less than RM4,000 per month • RM1,000 to HHs earning RM4,000–RM8,000 per month • RM800 to single individuals aged 21 years and above earning less than RM2,000 per month • RM500 to single individuals aged 21 years and above earning RM2,000–RM4,000 per month • Benefit as share of average HH income: 0.20 • Benefit as share of HH income of the lowest quintile: 0.69 • Benefit as share of average HH consumption expenditure: 0.35 • Benefit as share of HH consumption expenditure of the lowest quintile: 0.81	RM10 billion/ Part of second stimulus package of RM25 billion (1.7% of GDP)

continued on next page

Table A3.2 continued

	Timeliness		Coverage			Adequacy	Budget/ Cost/ Funding Source
Short Description	Date Announced	Date Implemented	Eligibility (Target Group/Fills social protection gap?)	Number of Beneficiaries	% Population	Benefit Amount	

Philippines

| Social Amelioration Program (SAP): linked to existing Pantawid Pamilyang Pilipino Program (4Ps) and Rice Subsidy | Cash transfers to 18 million low-income households with members in the informal market affected by the lockdown for 2 months (conditionality waived) | 24 Mar 2020 | 15 Apr 2020 | • Low-income households in areas under granular lockdown and households with recently returned overseas Filipino workers (OFWs)
 • Families qualified to receive the emergency subsidy should have at least one member who is a senior citizen, a person with disability, pregnant or lactating woman, solo parent, or overseas Filipino in distress
 • Households who are indigenous peoples or who belong to underprivileged and vulnerable sectors are also qualified to receive the emergency subsidy | • 4,353,597 existing plus 13,300,000
 • New: 4,353,597 | 16.9% plus 51.7% | • ₱5,000–₱8,000 ($248.52–$397.64 PPP) a month (depending on the prevailing regional minimum wage and considering the current conditional cash transfer grants and rice subsidies)

 • Benefit as share of average HH income: 0.30
 • Benefit as share of HH income of the lowest quintile: 0.72
 • Benefit as share of average HH consumption expenditure: 0.39
 • Benefit as share of HH consumption expenditure of the lowest quintile: 0.78
 • Extra benefit: $290 PPP (233% to 372%) | Not available |

continued on next page

Table A3.2 continued

		Timeliness		Coverage			Adequacy		Budget/ Cost/ Funding Source
	Short Description	Date Announced	Date Implemented	Eligibility (Target Group/Fills social protection gap?)	Number of Beneficiaries	% Population	Benefit Amount		
Emergency Subsidy Program (ESP) (new intervention)	Families and individuals affected by COVID-19, who did not qualify for SAP, received family food packs and nonfood items, including cash	19 Mar 2020	30 Mar 2020	• Families classified as low-income households by their local government units (LGUs) but were not qualified to receive SAP • LGUs that have requested for augmentation in support amid the enforcement of community quarantine due to the COVID-19 outbreak	• 628,243 non-4Ps families in Northern Mindanao (national level total to be verified) • Luzon: 49,039 received cash aid by 3 Jan 2021	Not available	• One-time cash grant of ₱5,000 to ₱8,000 ($248.52–$397.64 PPP) • 190,000 food packs in Luzon and 4,501,585 food packs and in Northern Mindanao • Benefit as share of average HH income: 0.30 • Benefit as share of HH income of the lowest quintile: 0.72 • Benefit as share of average HH consumption expenditure: 0.39 • Benefit as share of HH consumption expenditure of the lowest quintile: 0.78		₱1.3 billion/ Quick Response Fund from DSWD Central Office

continued on next page

Table A3.2 continued

	Timeliness		Coverage			Adequacy	Budget/Cost/Funding Source
Short Description	**Date Announced**	**Date Implemented**	**Eligibility** (Target Group/Fills social protection gap?)	**Number of Beneficiaries**	**% Population**	**Benefit Amount**	
Thailand							
Rao Chana	Low-income persons affected by the COVID-19 pandemic, mainly self-employed persons, farmers, and state welfare cardholders received weekly payments for 2 months	19 Jan 2021	18 Feb 2021 (Date of first payment for applicants who are current Pao Tang users and new applicants) / 5 Feb 2020 (Date of first payment for welfare card holders)	• Low-income persons affected by the COVID-19 pandemic, mainly self-employed persons, farmers, and state welfare cardholders. • Eligibility requirements: (1) Thai national, aged at least 18 years; (2) must not be insured under Section 33 of the Social Security Act; (3) must not be a government officer, government employee, state enterprise employee, political official, or people on a state pension. Applicants must have an annual income not exceeding B300,000 and bank savings not exceeding B500,000 (information will be checked back to 31 Dec 2019)	• 13,700,000 (existing welfare card holders) • New:[d] 21,500,000 • Welfare card holders: 13,700,000	19.7% plus 30.9%	• B3,500 ($271.88 PPP) per month for 2 months • Benefit as share of average HH income: 0.13 • Benefit as share of HH income of the lowest quintile: 0.45 • Benefit as share of average HH consumption expenditure: 0.17 • Increase from standard benefit: 338%	B213.24 billion / B210.20 billion (1st phase) plus B3.04 billion (extension approved on 20 April 2021)
Viet Nam							
Cash payments	Cash payments to vulnerable households, persons with meritorious services, and workers affected by the COVID-19 crisis	9 Apr 2020	1 Apr 2020	• Provisions for people with meritorious services to the revolution and beneficiaries of other social protection programs	• Previous recipients: 1,400,000 • Additional 8,400,000[c]	Going to 33.1%	• Poor and near poor HHs: D250,000/ person/month ($31.17 to $224.40 PPP) • Benefit as share of average HH income: 0.20 • Benefit as share of average HH consumption expenditure: 0.12	D36 trillion / Part of stimulus package of D62 trillion

continued on next page

Table A3.2 continued

Short Description	Timeliness		Coverage			Adequacy	Budget/ Cost/ Funding Source
	Date Announced	Date Implemented	Eligibility (Target Group/Fills social protection gap?)	Number of Beneficiaries	% Population	Benefit Amount	
			• Meritorious service eligibility: a) People who participated in the revolution before 1 January 1945; b) participated in the revolution from 1 January 1945 to before the General uprising of 19 August 1945; c) Martyrs; d) Vietnamese heroic mothers; e) People's Armed Forces Hero, Labor Hero; e) Invalids and policy beneficiaries such as war invalids; g) Diseases; h) Resistance activists are infected with toxic chemicals; i) People engaged in revolutionary activities and resistance activities were arrested and exiled by the enemy; k) People engaged in resistance war for national liberation, defense of the Fatherland and performing international obligations; l) People with meritorious services to the revolution; Relatives of persons with meritorious services to the revolution specified in Clause 1 of this Article Relatives of persons with meritorious services to the revolution specified in Clause 1 of this Article				

a Coverage expansion eligibility details not available.

b Cash transfer was provided for 3 months, and then extended for another 3 months, to poor persons living in villages or rural areas in Indonesia, mainly farmers. The BLT program aimed to maintain the purchasing power of persons living in villages affected by the COVID-19 crisis; 80% of the beneficiary families are low-income and have never received government assistance.

c Beneficiaries of the staple food card program received an additional transfer of Rp50,000 per month, a 25% increase relative to the standard benefit, through 9 basic commodity cards; by using the cards, the beneficiaries will be able to purchase and choose more diverse staple foods. [1] The budget increases to Rp1.80 million per family per annum from Rp1.32 million per family per annum in the previous year.

d Number of participants as of 22 April 2021 minus number of Welfare Card holders covered (13.7 million are holders of state Welfare Cards); 16.8 million are new applicants and persons whose information is already in the Pao Tang application, and 2.3 million are persons who need special assistance or those registering without smartphones. In April, budget was approved to cover an additional 2.4 million persons.

e Estimated coverage is 10 million (including 1.4 million persons with meritorious service and recipients of other social protection programs included as vertical expansion); 8.6 million for horizontal expansion.

Source: International Policy Centre for Inclusive Growth. 2021 Social Protection Responses to COVID-19 in the Global South. Mapping table. https://socialprotection.org/social-protection-responses-covid-19-global-south (accessed 9 November 2021).

Table A3.3: Social Insurance – Selected Policy Responses to COVID-19 in Southeast Asia

Short Description	Timeliness		Coverage			Adequacy	
	Date Announced	Date Implemented	Eligibility (Target Group/Fills social protection gap?)	Number of Beneficiaries	% Population or Labor Force	Benefit Amount	Budget/Cost/Funding Source
Indonesia							
Subsidized national health insurance (JKN) (linked to existing program)	18 May 2020	Not available	• National health insurance JKN) and BPJS Kesehatan (social security provider body). All Indonesian residents are required to become members of the National Health Insurance–Indonesian Health Cards (JKN-KIS) Program, managed by BPJS Kesehatan, including foreigners who have worked for at least 6 months in Indonesia and have paid dues • Poor persons, members of the JKN and BPJS identified as Class III patients, members classified as non-salaried employees (PBPU) and non-employees (BP) Class III	132,600,000	97%	Rp42,000 premiums per person ($8.03 PPP)	Rp33.3 trillion/Rp24.3 trillion financed by the federal government through allocation of state budget and Rp9 trillion financed by regional budget
Malaysia							
Employment Insurance System (EIS) — Eligibility criteria of the EIS was relaxed concerning the provision of unemployment benefits for retrenched workers in COVID-19 affected sectors, and the government increased the claimable training cost	23 Mar 2020	1 Apr 2020	• Malaysian citizens, permanent residents in Malaysia, aged 18–60 years, working in the private sector, and employed based on a contract of service	• 7,080,000 (in 2018) • Benefiting from intervention: 101,385	44% of labor force but only 0.6% of labor force benefiting from intervention	RM912,50 (daily training allowance of RM30) $538.10 PPP	Not available

continued on next page

Table A3.3 continued

	Timeliness		Coverage			Adequacy	
Short Description	Date Announced	Date Implemented	Eligibility (Target Group/Fills social protection gap?)	Number of Beneficiaries	% Population or Labor Force	Benefit Amount	Budget/Cost/Funding Source
• Training fee ceiling increased from RM4,000 to RM6,000, and trainees will be provided with a training allowance of RM30 per day			• Observations: Workers aged 57 years and above who have never paid contributions before that age are NOT covered by the EIS Act and are NOT required to contribute, the EIS Act does NOT cover domestic workers, the self-employed, civil servants, and workers in local authorities and statutory bodies				
I-Lestari Withdrawal (contributory pensions) • Employees Provident Fund (EPF) members can apply for early withdrawals of their own funds	12 Mar 2020	1 Apr 2020	• For EPF: Formal employees. Individuals who are employed, self-employed, or business owners can opt to contribute to the EPF based on their own requirements • For intervention: Malaysian citizens, permanent residents and non-Malaysians, 55 years old and below, have savings in Account 2	7,630,000 Benefiting from intervention: 3,510,000	48% of LF Benefiting from intervention: 22% of labor force	Maximum of RM500 per month ($294.85 PPP)	RM10 billion/ Employees Provident Fund

continued on next page

Table A3.3 continued

continued on next page

Philippines

| | | Timeliness | | Coverage | | | Adequacy | Budget/ |
| | | Date | Date | Eligibility | Number of | % Population | Benefit | Cost/Funding |
	Short Description	Announced	Implemented	(Target Group/Fills social protection gap?)	Beneficiaries	or Labor Force	Amount	Source
Unemployment benefits (SI)	Unemployment cash benefit for workers who lost their jobs due to the COVID-19 crisis	12 Mar 2020	12 Mar 2020	• Social Security System (SSS): Mandatory participation of private-sector employees, self-employed persons, and household workers • Voluntary coverage for citizens of the Philippines working abroad, persons who previously had mandatory coverage, and nonworking spouses of insured persons. • For intervention: Formal workers. Private sector workers rendered jobless by the COVID-19 pandemic, including HH helpers and OFWs who were laid off, terminated, or involuntary separated from their work. • Eligibility: The applicant must (i) be below 60 years old when they were removed from their job. For miners, they should be 50 years old or younger, while racehorse jockeys seeking the benefit must be aged 55 years or younger, (ii) have paid contributions to the SSS for at least 36 months, with at least 12 payments remitted in the last 18 months before they were booted out of work, (iii) not have received an unemployment benefit in the past 3 years when he/she applied for the perk	18,360,000 million SSS members in 2018 Benefiting from intervention: 60,000	40% of labor force Benefiting from intervention: 0.1% of labor force	• Half of the worker's average monthly salary, up to ₱20,000 ($994.08 PPP). The average value is ₱11,000 • 38% of per capita GDP • 136% of average salary	₱1.2 billion/ Department of Labor and Employment

Table A3.3 continued

continued on next page

	Timeliness		Coverage			Adequacy	Budget/
Short Description	**Date Announced**	**Date Implemented**	**Eligibility** (Target Group/Fills social protection gap?)	**Number of Beneficiaries**	**% Population or Labor Force**	**Benefit Amount**	**Cost/Funding Source**
Thailand							
Unemployment benefits (Force majeure) — Unemployment benefits for COVID–19 related contingencies affecting workers insured under the SSF	17 Apr 2020	31 Mar 2020	• Workers are insured and eligible to receive unemployment benefits: have to cease working temporarily between 1 Mar and 31 Aug 2020; do not receive wages from the employer during the temporary cessation; and, whose employment has not been terminated. • Workers in the following force majeure circumstances are eligible: The employee has to cease working because they are required to quarantine or comply with a COVID–19 preventive measure. The employer orders the cessation of the employee's work because the employer has to quarantine the employee, or the employer has to comply with a COVID–19 preventive measure. • Force majeure causes the employer to temporarily cease normal business operations, partially or wholly, because they decide to do so, or must do so to comply with an order in accordance with laws relating to communicable diseases or emergency public administration	New program beneficiaries 984,005	2.5% of labor force	• 62% of the monthly salary for up to 90 days, subject to an eligible monthly salary cap of B15,000; B9,300 per month ($629.42 PPP) • 45% of per capita GDP • 61.2% of average wage	Not available

Table A3.3 continued

	Short Description	Timeliness		Coverage			Adequacy	
		Date Announced	Date Implemented	Eligibility (Target Group/Fills social protection gap?)	Number of Beneficiaries	Population or Labor Force %	Benefit Amount	Budget/Cost/Funding Source
Unemployment benefits (Economic crisis)	Insured employees under the SSF are entitled to receive benefits during periods of unemployment caused by the economic crisis between 1 Mar 2020 and 28 Feb 2022	17 Apr 2020	31 Mar 2020	Insured workers under the SSF who are unemployed between 1 Mar 2020 and 28 Feb 2022, and who have paid contributions for at least 6 of the prior 15 months counted from the date of unemployment	15,224 new beneficiaries	0.03% of labor force	• If employee is terminated: 70% of daily wages for up to 200 days; if employee resigns or their contract ends: 45% of daily wage for up to 3 months • Maximum daily wage is capped at B15,000 per month (B10,500 for up to 200 days; B6,750 for 3 months) • Max amount $710.64 PPP • 72% of per capita GDP • 69.1% of average wages	Not available
Viet Nam								
Health Care for COVID-19 patients	Health Insurance Fund (HIF) Free care for persons (national and foreigners) under mandatory quarantine at isolation facilities	13 Mar 2020	13 Mar 2020	• COVID-19 patients in the country, nationals and foreigners • Targeting: Vulnerable individuals (children, elderly, disabled, refugees, internally displaced persons – not related to work, but to vulnerability)	83,922,036 (coverage if HIF in 2018) 1,521 actual beneficiaries (total number of cases in Viet Nam) by Jan 2021	87% of population <0.1% population		Part of the D6.7 trillion stage budget

Source: International Policy Centre for Inclusive Growth. 2021 Social Protection Responses to COVID-19 in the Global South. Mapping table. https://socialprotection.org/social-protection-responses-covid-19-global-south (accessed 9 November 2021).

References

Asian Development Bank (ADB). 2020. *COVID-19 Active Response and Expenditure Support Program.* Employment and Poverty Assessment: Cambodia. https://www.adb.org/sites/default/files/linked-documents/54195-001-sd-03.pdf.

_____. 2021a. *Asian Development Outlook (ADO) 2021 Update.* Manila.

_____. 2021b. Supporting Post-COVID-19 Economic Recovery in Southeast Asia. ADB Briefs. No. 175. Manila.

_____. 2021c. *Technical and Vocational Education and Training in the Philippines in the Age of Industry 4.0.* Manila.

ADB Institute, Organisation for Economic Co-operation and Development (OECD), and International Labour Organization (ILO). 2021. *Labor Migration in Asia: Impacts of the COVID-19 Crisis and the Post-Pandemic Future.* https://www.adb.org/sites/default/files/publication/690751/adbi-book-labor-migration-asia-impacts-covid-19-crisis-post-pandemic-future.pdf.

Barrero, J. M., N. Bloom, S. J. Davis, and B. H. Meyer. 2021. COVID-19 Is a Persistent Reallocation Shock. *American Economic Association Papers and Proceedings.* 111 (May 2021). pp. 287–91.

Beazley, R., M. Marzi, and R. Steller. 2021. *Drivers of Timely and Large-Scale Cash Responses to COVID19: What Does the Data Say?* May. Social Protection Approaches to COVID-19 Expert Advice Service (SPACE). United Kingdom: DAI Global UK Ltd. https://socialprotection.org/sites/default/files/publications_files/SPACE_Drivers%20of%20Timely%20and%20Large%20Scale%20Cash%20Responses%20to%20COVID_19%20%281%29.pdf.

Benes, E. M. and K. Walsh. 2018. Measuring Unemployment and the Potential Labour Force in Labour Force Surveys: Main Findings from the ILO LFS Pilot Studies. *Statistical Methodology Series.* Geneva: ILO. https://www.ilo.org/wcmsp5/groups/public/---dgreports/---stat/documents/publication/wcms_627878.pdf.

Charoensuthipan, P. 2021. Over 650,000 Workers Seek Amnesty as Govt Sounds Warning. *Bangkok Post.* 15 February. https://www.bangkokpost.com/thailand/general/2068151/over-650-000-workers-seek-amnesty-as-govt-sounds-warning.

Coordinating Ministry for Economic Affairs of the Republic of Indonesia. 2021. *Kartu Prakerja Program Management Report 2020.* Jakarta. https://static-asset-cdn.prakerja.go.id/www/ebook-reporting/Kartu_Prakerja_Program_Management_Report_2020_New.pdf.

De La Fuente, A. 2011. New Measures of Labour Market Attachment: 3 New Eurostat Indicators to Supplement the Unemployment Rate. Eurostat – Statistics in Focus 57/2011. https://ec.europa.eu/eurostat/documents/3433488/5579744/KS-SF-11-057-EN.PDF.

Durán-Valverde, F., J. F. Pacheco-Jimenez, T. Muzaffar, and H. Elizondo-Barboza. 2020. Financing Gaps in Social Protection: Global Estimates and Strategies for Developing Countries in Light of the COVID-19 Crisis and Beyond. *International Labour Organization Working Paper.* 14. October. Geneva: ILO.

Economic and Social Commission for Asia and the Pacific (ESCAP) and International Labour Organization (ILO). 2020. *Asia-Pacific Migration Report 2020: Assessing Implementation of the Global Compact for Migration.* Bangkok.

_____. 2021a. *Social Protection Responses to COVID-19 in Asia and the Pacific: The Story So Far and Future Considerations.* https://www.ilo.org/wcmsp5/groups/public/---asia/---ro-bangkok/documents/publication/wcms_753550.pdf.

_____. 2021b. *The Protection We Want Social Outlook for Asia and the Pacific.* Bangkok.

European Parliament. 2021. Post Covid-19 Value Chains: Options for Reshoring Production Back to Europe in a Globalized Economy. Policy Department for External Relations. https://www.europarl.europa.eu/thinktank/en/document.html?reference=EXPO_STU(2021)653626.

Generalao, I. N. A. 2021. Measuring the telework potential of jobs: evidence from the International Standard Classification of Occupations. *Philippine Review of Economics.* 58(1&2): 92-127. DOI:10.37907/5ERP1202JD.

Gentilini, U. et al. 2021. *Social Protection and Jobs Responses to COVID-19: A Real-Time Review of Country Measures.* COVID-19 Living Paper. Washington, DC: World Bank Group.

Google, Temasek, and Bain. 2020. e-Conomy SEA 2020: At Full Velocity — Resilient and Racing Ahead.

Heller, P. 2005. Understanding Fiscal Space. IMF Policy Discussion Paper. No. PDP/05/4. Washington, DC: International Monetary Fund.

International Labour Organization (ILO). 2017. *World Social Protection Report 2017–19: Universal Social Protection to Achieve the Sustainable Development Goals.* Geneva.

_____. 2020a. *ILO Monitor: COVID-19 and the World of Work. Fifth Edition.* 30 June. https://www.ilo.org/wcmsp5/groups/public/---dgreports/---dcomm/documents/briefingnote/wcms_749399.pdf.

_____. 2020b. *ILO Monitor: COVID-19 and the World of Work. Sixth Edition.* 23 September. https://www.ilo.org/wcmsp5/groups/public/---dgreports/---dcomm/documents/briefingnote/wcms_755910.pdf.

_____. 2020c. Gendered Impacts of COVID-19 on the Garment Sector. November. ILO Brief. Geneva.

_____. 2020d. *Social Protection Responses to COVID-19 in Asia and the Pacific: The Story so Far and Future Considerations.* Bangkok. https://www.ilo.org/asia/publications/WCMS_753550/lang--en/index.htm.

_____. 2020e. *Asia-Pacific Employment and Social Outlook: Navigating the Crisis towards a Human-Centered Future of Work.* Bangkok.

_____. 2020f. Protecting Migrant Workers during the COVID-19 Pandemic: Recommendations for Policy-Makers and Constituents. ILO Policy Brief. https://www.ilo.org/wcmsp5/groups/public/---ed_protect/---protrav/---migrant/documents/publication/wcms_743268.pdf.

_____. 2020g. Experiences of ASEAN Migrant Workers during COVID-19: Rights at Work, Migration and Quarantine during the Pandemic, and Re-Migration Plans. ILO Brief. https://www.ilo.org/wcmsp5/groups/public/---asia/---ro-bangkok/documents/briefingnote/wcms_746881.pdf.

_____. 2020h. COVID-19: Impact on Migrant Workers and Country Response in Thailand. Briefing Note. 3 July. https://www.ilo.org/wcmsp5/groups/public/---asia/---ro-bangkok/---sro-bangkok/documents/briefingnote/wcms_741920.pdf.

_____. 2020i. *World Economic and Social Outlook – Trends 2020.* Geneva.

_____. 2021a. *World Economic and Social Outlook – Trends 2021*. Geneva.

_____. 2021b. *ILO Monitor: COVID-19 and the World of Work. Seventh Edition.* 25 January. https://www.ilo.org/wcmsp5/groups/public/---dgreports/---dcomm/documents/briefingnote/wcms_767028.pdf.

_____. 2021c. COVID-19, Vaccinations and Consumer Demand: How Jobs Are Affected through Global Supply Chains?. June. ILO Brief. Geneva.

_____. 2021d. COVID-19 and the ASEAN Labour Market: Impact and Policy Response. August. ILO Brief. Geneva.

_____. 2021e. Supporting Migrant Workers During the Pandemic for a Cohesive and Responsive ASEAN Community. Thematic Background Paper for the 13th ASEAN Forum on Migrant Labour. http://www.ilo.int/wcmsp5/groups/public/---asia/---ro-bangkok/---sro-bangkok/documents/publication/wcms_816971.pdf.

_____. 2021f. *World Social Protection Report 2020–22: Social Protection at the Crossroads – in Pursuit of a Better Future*. Geneva.

_____. Forthcoming. *World Economic and Social Outlook – Trends 2022*. Geneva.

International Monetary Fund (IMF). 2021a. Fiscal Monitor Database of Country Fiscal Measures in Response to the COVID-19 Pandemic. https://www.imf.org/en/Topics/imf-and-covid19/Fiscal-Policies-Database-in-Response-to-COVID-19 (accessed 3 May 2021).

_____. 2021b. *World Economic Outlook Update.* Washington, DC.

Kar, D. and J. Spanjers. 2015. Illicit Financial Flows from Developing Countries: 2004–2013. Global Financial Integrity. https://secureservercdn.net/50.62.198.97/34n.8bd.myftpupload.com/wp-content/uploads/2015/12/IFF-Update_2015-Final-1.pdf.

Khamis, M., D. Prinz, D. Newhouse, A. Palacios-Lopez, U. Pape, and M. Weber. 2021. The Early Labor Market Impacts of COVID-19 in Developing Countries: Evidence from High-Frequency Phone Surveys. *Jobs Working Paper*. Issue No. 58. Washington, DC: World Bank. https://openknowledge.worldbank.org/bitstream/handle/10986/35044/The-Early-Labor-Market-Impacts-of-COVID-19-in-Developing-Countries-Evidence-from-High-frequency-Phone-Surveys.pdf?sequence=6&isAllowed=y.

Kose, M. A., S. Kurlat, F. Ohnsorge, and N. Sugawara. 2017. A Cross-Country Database of Fiscal Space. *Policy Research Working Paper*. No. 8157. Washington, DC: World Bank.

Ley, E. 2009. Fiscal Policy for Growth. PREM Notes. No. 131. Washington, DC: World Bank.

Mazumdaru, S. 2021. COVID Surge in Southeast Asia Disrupts Global Supply Chains. 9 September. *Deutsche Welle (DW)*. https://www.dw.com/en/covid-surge-in-southeast-asia-disrupts-global-supply-chains/a-59062324.

Megersa, K. 2019. Lessons Learned from Linking Social Protection to Tax Revenue. K4D Helpdesk Report 717. Brighton, UK: Institute of Development Studies. https://opendocs.ids.ac.uk/opendocs/handle/20.500.12413/14986.

Morgan, P. J. and L. Q. Trinh. 2021. Impacts of COVID-19 on Households in ASEAN Countries and their Implications for Human Capital Development. *ADBI Working Paper Series*. No. 1226. Tokyo: ADB Institute.

Müller, C., B. Graf, K. Pfeiffer, S. Bieller, N. Kutzbach, and K. Röhricht. 2020. *World Robotics 2020 – Service Robots*. Frankfurt am Main, Germany: IFR Statistical Department, VDMA Services GmbH.

Oikawa, K. et al. 2021. The Impact of COVID-19 on Business Activities and Supply Chains in the ASEAN Member States and India. *ERIA Discussion Paper Series.* No. 384. Jakarta: Economic Research Institute for ASEAN and East Asia (ERIA).

Ortiz, I., A. Chowdhury, F. Durán-Valverde, T. Muzaffar, and S. Urban 2019. *Fiscal Space for Social Protection. A Handbook for Assessing Financing Options.* Geneva: ILO.

Ostry, J. D., A. R. Ghosh, J. I. Kim, and M. S. Qureshi. 2010. Fiscal Space. IMF Staff Position Note. SPN/10/11. Washington, DC: IMF.

Patinio, F. 2021. Gov't Distributes P10.5-B under DOLE's Employment Programs. *Philippine News Agency.* 31 August. https://www.pna.gov.ph/articles/1152157.

Perotti, R. 2007. Fiscal Policy in Developing Countries: A Framework and Some Questions. *Policy Research Working Paper.* No. 4365. Washington, DC: .

Philippine Statistics Authority (PSA). 2020 . Total Number of OFWs Estimated at 2.2 Million. https://psa.gov.ph/statistics/survey/labor-and-employment/survey-overseas-filipinos (accessed 12 August 2021).

Ricchetti, M. and R. D. Palma. 2020. Will COVID-19 Accelerate the Transition to a Sustainable Fashion Industry?. United Nations Industrial Development Organization. 9 October. https://www.unido.org/stories/will-covid-19-accelerate-transition-sustainable-fashion-industrySrinivas, S. and S. Sivaraman. 2020. Understanding Relevant Sustainable Development Goal Targets Related to Labour Migration in the Association of Southeast Asian Nations During the Coronavirus Disease Pandemic. *ERIA Research Project Report 2021.* No. 04. Jakarta: ERIA. https://www.eria.org/uploads/media/Research-Project-Report/RPR-2021-04/Understanding-Relevant-Sustainable-Development-Goal-Targets-Related-to-Labour-Migration-in-ASEAN-During-COVID-19.pdf

TESDA. 2021a. Free Access to TESDA's Online Skills Training Program Extended Until 2022. 27 April. https://www.tesda.gov.ph/News/Details/20007.

TESDA. 2021b. TESDA Online Program 2021 Monitoring Report from January to September 2021.

Theparat, C., W. Chantanusornsiri, and M. Bangprapa. 2021. Govt Approves COVID Handouts. *Bangkok Post.* 3 January. https://www.bangkokpost.com/thailand/general/2049843/govt-approves-covid-handouts.

United Nations (UN). 2020. Shared Responsibility, Global Solidarity: Responding to the Socio-Economic Impacts of COVID-19. https://unsdg.un.org/sites/default/files/2020-03/SG-Report-Socio-Economic-Impact-of-Covid19.pdf.

United Nations, Economic and Social Commission for Asia and the Pacific (ESCAP). 2020. *Asia-Pacific Migration Report 2020: Assessing Implementation of the Global Compact for Migration.* Bangkok. https://www.unescap.org/sites/default/files/APMR2020_FullReport.pdf.

United Nations World Tourism Organization (UNWTO). 2020. Tourism in SIDS: The Challenge of Sustaining Livelihoods in Times of COVID-19. UNWTO Briefing Note – Tourism and COVID-19. Issue 2. Madrid. DOI: https://doi.org/10.18111/9789284421916.

_____. 2021a. World Tourism Barometer Statistical Annex. Volume 19 (Issue 4). July. Madrid.

_____. 2021b. World Tourism Barometer Statistical Annex. Volume 19. Issue 3. May. Madrid.

World Bank. The Atlas of Social Protection – Indicators of Resilience and Equity. https://databank.worldbank.org/source/1229 (accessed 7 May 2021).

_____. 2020. *Poverty and Shared Prosperity 2020: Reversals of Fortune.* Washington, DC.

_____. 2021. *Towards Social Protection 4.0: An Assessment of Thailand's Social Protection and Labor Market Systems.* Bangkok: World Bank.

_____. 2021b. Thailand Economic Monitor: The Road to Recovery July 2021. Bangkok: World Bank.

_____. 2021c. Long COVID. *World Bank East Asia and Pacific Economic Update October 2021.* Washington, DC.

www.ingramcontent.com/pod-product-compliance
Lightning Source LLC
Chambersburg PA
CBHW042033220326
41599CB00045BA/7294